THE ATHLETE'S GUIDE TO
SPORTS PSYCHOLOGY:
MENTAL SKILLS FOR PHYSICAL PEOPLE

DEDICATION

This book is dedicated to our parents,
who were always there to support our
involvement in sport and who taught us
many of the skills and strategies we
share with our readers.

THE ATHLETE'S GUIDE TO
SPORTS
PSYCHOLOGY:
MENTAL SKILLS FOR PHYSICAL PEOPLE

DOROTHY V. HARRIS, Ph.D.
BETTE L. HARRIS, Ed.D.

LEISURE PRESS

CHAMPAIGN ILLINOIS

A publication of
Leisure Press
A division of Human Kinetics Publishers, Inc.
Box 5076, Champaign, IL 61820
Copyright © 1984 Leisure Press
All rights reserved. Printed in the U.S.A.

Library of Congress Catalog Card Number: 83-807-35

ISBN: 0-88011-206-9

Cover and book design: Brian Groppe
Layout and Production: John Jett
Cover photo: David Madison

*All photos by Jim O'Hara, Carolyn Wells and Nancy Andrews, except for those
noted below:
Dick Broussard, Colgate University: 146
Phil Diggingee: 160
Exertrail, Inc.: 60
Don Gosney: 94, 164
Charles Lips: 14
Bill Miller, St. Louis Community College: 131
Stanford University Department of Athletics: 130
UCLA Athletic Department: 83
University of California Department of Women's Athletics: 76
University of Pittsburgh Department of Athletics: 173
Richard Zoeller: 178

CONTENTS

PREFACE

There is probably not one of us who has not "choked" at some point in athletics, or blown our lines on stage, or blanked out on an exam, or created a problem for ourselves because we were trying too hard. Usually when we try harder, we increase our arousal which can become counter-productive.

There is a great deal of discussion about stress in today's society with most of the discussion focusing on the distressful aspects. However, stress is the thing that gets our juices flowing. It is the response to some type of external stress, either real or perceived. The pulse that speeds up, the breathing rate which changes, the clammy hands, and all the other alarm signals can be lifesaving in a true emergency. The fact is, many of us experience these alarm responses on a fairly regular basis in situations that are not life threatening.

Stress is not necessarily bad; it prods us into action. Stress-inducing events can even be pleasurable experiences, particularly in sport. The "bad stress" or that which causes distress is actually arousal out of control. Once that happens, everything begins to fall apart resulting in a general state of confusion and dysfunction. Yet arousal does not have to get out of control. Some of us thrive on controlling our arousal and intentionally subject ourselves to situations that will provide us with an opportunity to cope. Without the challenge of controlling and regulating our responses in these situations, we would become lazy and bored. We need stress to keep us alert and productive.

Competitive sport provides an ideal laboratory for teaching us how to cope with situations that create worry and anxiety about how well we perform. We hear a lot about competitive stress in sport these days. There are long arguments about the pros and cons of competitive sport for youth. Competition is an integral part of free enterprise and of a capitalistic society. Youth sports may provide the best laboratory for teaching youngsters early on how to control and regulate their worries and anxieties so they can maximize their potential. After all, most youngsters start out enjoying their participation in sport. They are highly motivated to learn and to practice skills and strategies that will help them get better. These coping skills and strategies that work for them in sport can also be applied to all other situations throughout life which cause worry, anxiety and stress. In fact, competitive sport provides the first and best opportunity to teach youngsters how to cope with stress.

Many argue that competitive sport is big business and should be taken out of the educational system. Competitive sport can be educational if it takes place within the framework of education. Competitive sport can provide great opportunity for teaching personal growth and the development of skills and strategies relevant to the situation in which they are taught. These same coping skills and strategies will last a lifetime as the principles of coping with stress are the same whether it be competitive stress, deadline pressures, disagreements with co-workers, threats of self-esteem in personal or career situations, threats of job loss, or whatever. With all the concern about the undesirable effects of chronic or long-term stress, learning to cope may be the best lesson we can teach youngsters. It will contribute to maximizing their potential as well as enhancing well-being.

Just think of the magnitude of the contribution to society that teaching cognitive skills and strategies to all youth through sport programs could make. Think how much more helpful it would be if all coaches and teachers of sport understood the integrated mechanisms that underline arousal, worry and anxiety and could apply that knowledge in situations that are relevant and meaningful to the learner. Picture the way sport performance could be if every aspect, every participant; athlete, coach trainer, and spectator; had a broad understanding of the integrated, holistic workings of the physical and mental processes necessary to attain one's potential in any pursuit.

The emphasis would be on the athlete's own capacity and ability to feel and to experience what is going on in his or her body, to experience cognitively and physically in a fine-tuned, integrated manner what involvement in exercise and sport is all about. The focus would be on the athlete's own internal state as a function of performance in every endeavor, sport or otherwise.

The athlete would become a conscious participant in the process of learning how to tune in to his or her body, read the signals, and regulate them to maximize the potential there . This approach places heavy emphasis on self-awareness and on the individual assuming responsibilities for his or her own arousal and control under all conditions. This approach would provide creative insight into how to extend the limits of our abilities.

Only in sport and physical education within the formal educational structure is the opportunity provided to teach each and every individual how to integrate in an holistic manner both physical and cognitive awareness in such a way that each can become all that he or she is capable of becoming. This places physical education, exercise and competitive sport firmly within the educational arena.

The major role of sport psychology education is teaching cognitive skills and strategies to sports participants. It has little to do with providing therapy or treating social dysfunction. It has become increasingly obvious that those who know and understand sport are in a much better position to teach and to learn these skills than those who are trained in the psychological skills but do not have a broad-based knowledge of the sport sciences and of the behavior demands made on the athlete in competitive sport situations. Coaches and athletes can be taught the principles of coping strategies and skills. However, it is almost impossible to teach the concepts of competitive sport to psychologists who have been trained in behavioral strategies and skills but who have had little or no experience in a variety of competitive sports. As a result, those who know sport (athletes and coaches in particular) are in a much better position to learn and to teach mental skills and strategies to control and regulate arousal in order to maximize performance. In the final analysis, either the coach or the athlete is the one who should be incorporating the psychological skills and strategies in practice and preparation for competition. Only in a rare instance will a professionally trained psychologist ever be needed to work with an athlete. When these situations occur, the coach can refer the athlete for professional help.

This book is written for those of you (coach or athlete) who desire to maximize your potential in sport performance. One of the largest omissions in sport skills training has been that of recognizing the mind/body or mental/physical integration necessary for learning. Traditionally repetition has been stressed as the only way to maximize skill performance. Cognitive aspects of performance were focused on the strategic components, not on individual performance as such. Incorporating both the mental and physical aspects of skill performance is long overdue.

If you are motivated to improve your performance and to become a better athlete, this book will provide concepts, understandings, skills and strategies so that you can accomplish that goal. It will take time and effort on your part as there are no shortcuts to improving athletic performance. The prescriptions offered here are not magical nor are they cure alls. They are, however, procedures which allow you to enter competition knowing that you control your behavior and your performance outcomes.

The mental aspects of performance can not be separated from the physical; your training must be holistic. That is the approach of this book. It is assumed you already understand the mechanics of specific sport skills and the principles of physical training. We go beyond the traditional approach to preparing for competition by explaining how the mental and physical aspects are integrated and how you think with your muscles. Once you understand holistic and integrated response you are ready to learn about the relationship of anxiety and performance and how dysfunction can result if you do not become aware of this relationship and learn to regulate your arousal to avoid interference in your performance.

When this concept is understood you are ready to develop an awareness of things you may be doing that tend to interfere and prevent you from attaining your potential performance. First you need to become aware of your self-thoughts, mental barriers and mind sets that become self-fulfilling prophecies for your performance. In general, it is our perceptions and thoughts that get us into trouble. When they are negative and self-defeating they generate worry which leads to anxiety and tension. Relaxation is the best antidote for that state. Several different approaches to relaxation are included with directions for developing the skills.

After you have learned to relax sufficiently to reduce the interference in both initiating and responding to stimulation, you are ready to learn how to improve your concentration skills. Strategies and exercises are included which will help you increase your ability to direct your attention and to regain your concentration when you have a mental lapse.

When you can keep your thoughts positive and constructive, relax away unnecessary tension, and maintain concentration without having your thoughts wander all over the place, you are ready to develop the skills of using your imagination or to mentally visualize and rehearse everything that you can do physically. In fact, you can learn to mentally prepare for situations you cannot structure physically for practice. Just think of the potential that holds for preparation for competition!

Goal setting strategies are presented next as a means of regulating your motivation and sustaining effort over time. You will learn how to set specific goals that are measurable so you will know when you attain them. Applying goal setting strategies to your practice and performance situations will serve to enhance your enjoyment and satisfaction of sport involvement.

Inasmuch as sport generally takes place in a social situation, communication becomes an important skill to acquire. You will learn how to become more aware of all types and levels of communication and how you can improve your skills of both receiving and sending communication signals.

In nearly every pursuit there are roadblocks, setbacks and obstacles to overcome. A discussion of many of those that athletes encounter is included so you can become more aware of them and understand what is happening when you do experience one.

Finally, you are presented with some questionnaires, check lists and exercises you can use to determine where you are with regard to an awareness of how you cope with competitive stress. You can use these to periodically check the progress you make toward gaining more self-regulation and control over your arousal. Hopefully, you will discover the best way to monitor your progress toward reaching your potential performance will be keeping a daily record of everything that contributes or interferes with your performance.

This book has evolved through years of competitive athletic experience and coaching. Bette L. Harris made significant contributions to the chapters on goal setting, communication and overcoming obstacles. Beyond those chapters, the experience that Dorothy V. Harris has had in sport psychology education in developing one of the first graduate programs in sport psychology and coordinating those efforts since the 1960's has provided a wealth of knowledge from which to draw. That has been enhanced by spending a sabbatical leave working with athletes at the Olympic Training Center in Colorado Springs and teaching a course, Inner Sports to competitive athletes at Penn State University for several years. In so doing, the athletes have served as her teachers regarding their worries, concerns, needs and desires. Gratitude is extended to each and every athlete and coach with whom we have worked. This book would never have become a reality without their cooperation, willingness to experiment, their evaluation of what worked and what did not, and the sharing of their insight into other ways to improve their performance once they learned the basic skills and strategies. Their interest in improving their own sport performance has challenged our thinking as well as our methodology.

We wish to acknowledge the photographic contributions of Jim O'Hara, sports editor of the Farmville Herald and Carolyn Wells and Nancy Andrews of Longwood College. Their keen insight and understanding of the components of sport performance is clearly captured in their work.

1

THINKING WITH YOUR MUSCLES: THE MIND/BODY INTEGRATION

How do you learn to be a consistent performer? How do you learn to maximize your performance within your own genetic, physiological or biomechanical boundaries? Is physical practice the only component included in your training program? We "think with our muscles" but when it comes to determining how we are going to improve our performance or attain consistency in performance, practice repetition has been our only answer. We try harder, however, it does not always produce the desired results.

Thinking with our muscles! Certainly not a new concept but one which we have neglected putting into practice. To be a better athlete does not necessarily mean that you must train harder or longer. It could mean that you need to address all the components that make up an athletic performance, those being physical as well as mental. It means assessing which facets you have overlooked or ignored in your preparation and training. Since you do not enter competition without your head, you must plan to include mental skills in your training and conditioning programs. This means developing strategies which allow you to enter competition with the proper mindset and which will enable you to perform at your most consistent and highest level. If you are interested in getting the most out of your athletic endeavors, you can no longer treat your performance as a combination of isolated factors which come together in some mysterious and unified way on the day of the competition. You would never think to enter a long distance race without spending time physically preparing your body to meet the conditioning demands of the race. Yet, you probably enter the race without determining what psychological skills you need to help achieve your best physical performance. Almost no one prepares and practices the necessary mental conditioning.

What do we mean when we say "That athlete has got it together?" What is there to get together? A science of athletic performance is evolving. With that comes an increasing body of knowledge and an increasing awareness of the necessity of integrating the mental and physical aspects of performance. Traditionally, coaches and athletes have devoted most of their attention to the physical components of performance. Practices have focused on the skills, techniques, and strategies involved in sport or how to use x's and o's to win. Almost no attention has been given to the cognitive aspects of performance. Yet, attributions given by the coaches and athletes for not performing up to expectations generally involve those related to the mental aspects of performance! "They weren't hungry enough," "We lost our momentum," "I got psyched out," "I just didn't want it enough," or "I wasn't psyched enough" are comments frequently used to describe competitive disappointments. Rarely do you find a coach who says that the team has not been taught the proper psychological skills and strategies. An athlete seldom concludes a loss was related to poor or inadequate preparation of psychological strategies. However, after the game, the greatest percentage of excuses are generally attributed to the mental and emotional aspects of the game. Yet, almost no time is spent in incorporating these into the training routine. Usually it is back to the drawing board for a new strategy or increased practice time.

It is becoming obvious that outstanding athletes differ from their teammates who do not perform as well. The physiological and biomechanical differences among these athletes are much better understood than the cognitive differences because research and attention has been devoted to those considerations in performance. It is much easier to evaluate cardiovascular or mechanical differences between athletes than it is to evaluate different athletic "mindsets" about performance. This point is best underscored when trying to understand why two athletes with identical qualifying times in track and field do not have the same finishing times. Why is it that performances differ on given days or even in the same event? Only recently, in the late 1970s and early 1980s, have we turned our attention to the mental and emotional training of athletes as a part of their preparation for maximizing performance outcomes.

Just as the principles of exercise physiology, sports medicine, and biomechanics have to be employed to enhance performance, so do the principles of psychological preparation.

Acknowledging your potential performance is limited by your genetic, physiological and biomechanical capabilities, the task becomes one of how to maximize your performance to the upper limits within those boundaries. In other words, consistent performance will depend on how you learn to regulate your cognitive skills during the competition.

The fact that many athletes display a high level of performance during practice but fail to maintain that same level of skill production during competition gives cause for concern. One might speculate some teams practice turnovers when you watch them in competition because they execute them with such consistent skill! If turnovers are not a part of one's practice but become a part of the competitive performance, the coach must begin to assess the reason for the turnovers and find ways of eliminating them. Improving performance is not accomplished by isolating the body from the mind, even if that were possible! Improving performance, in this case eliminating turnovers, involves training the whole individual. This includes providing cognitive skills and strategies that deal with skilled performance as well as including physical performance skills. Turnovers caused by small mental errors of poor timing, misreading relevant cues or failure to attend to a specific play will not be corrected solely by repetition of passing drills.

In general, there is no marked change in your physiological capacity or in your skill level or biomechanical efficiency during a competition or between two competitions which immediately follow each other. What does change is psychological control — your MINDSET! When a team or individual loses momentum, or gains momentum, the change is created by psychological factors. You do not suddenly lose or gain stamina, skill, strategy, or conditioning during a competition. However, you can gain or lose psychological control or get psyched out over the time span of a competition. When you "choke" in a close competitive situation, your psychological frame of reference interferes with your skill production.

The fluctuation in psychological regulation can be prevented, thus avoiding performance decrements by developing coping skills and strategies to manage anxiety or worry about performance. You must be taught or assume responsibility for learning your own arousal mechanisms and to perform under control, establishing behaviors which allow you to perform in a consistent manner. You cannot expect the coach, or cheerleaders, or the fans to provide the stimulus for your arousal or to assist in the controlling of your psychological mindset for performance. You are as responsible for your arousal regulation as you are responsible for maintaining a proper diet, for getting sufficient rest, and for training to maximize physiological and/or biochemical capabilities.

While it is easier to observe the shifts in momentum among athletes who participate in individual sports, similar situations occur in team sports. Within a single competition, a wide fluctuation of performance can be observed. A team can dominate the first half of a match and fail to maintain that same level of performance during the second half. Frequently a single play can be identified that may have created the shift in momentum. These changes in momentum are not usually precipitated by physiological or biochemical shifts, or by a sudden reduction in skill and ability, BUT by inconsistent psychological regulation of the cognitive skills and strategies that are essential for maximizing and maintaining a consistenly high level of performance.

The general knowledge of coaches and athletes concerning strategies and techniques for psychological training is virtually nonexistent. Most of us are aware of the need, yet do little about rectifying it because we do not know what to do! As a result, we have become vulnerable to superstitions, rituals, and other means of trying to incorporate some type of regular routine into our preparation for competition. We resort to ranting and raving with our inability and frustration in trying to deal with inconsistent performance and failure to perform in competition as executed in practice.

We have become vulnerable to gimmicks and fads that are always around practice fields and locker rooms and use them as lmethods to improve performance. The Dallas Cowboys Football team probably has been more scientific in their draft selection and in their training than most other professional or amateur teams. Feeling the next breakthrough in maximizing performance was psychological, they have pursued that route. While one might question the use of commercially produced tanks filled with warm salt water for producing relaxation, one has to give the Cowboys credit for taking the initiative in the psychological training of their athletes. Other teams have pursued similar routes. The Oakland Athletics Baseball team hired an astrologer to help them in preparation. The Toronto Maple Leafs ice hockey team used a pyramid structure to generate energy for the Stanley Cup competitions. The following year the Maple Leafs resorted to spraying negative ions to improve their chance in the Stanley Cup playoffs. Still other athletes have resorted to hypnosis or to related behavioral procedures to improve performance. There appears to be little concern about whether or not there is any evidence these approaches work. The significant factor in all of this is the demonstrated need for some assistance in filling the void of expertise among athletes and coaches in the psychological preparation. We know that practice repetition and increased physical conditioning have failed to bring about consistently high performances so there must be some other approach that is needed.

Many ridiculous pursuits of consistent performance exist among the circle of the elite athletes. This a sad commentary on the psychological science of competitive preparation. Coaches as well as athletes become vulnerable to any and every promise of some help, even to those "peddling snake oil." We need to be educated as to what causes inconsistent performances and as to what we might do to prevent these decrements in performance. As the awareness and recognition of psychological training increases, it becomes obvious that all training programs should incorporate psychological principles with the same emphasis and degree as those placed on physiological and biomechanical principles. Learning psychological skills and stategies is of parallel importance in the pusuit of consistent performance.

It takes time to develop and optimize individual behavioral skills necessary to maximize athletic performance. A rainy day plan or a one day lecture will not do it any more effectively than a one time discussion of a physical skill or strategy involved in athletic performance. What is required is practice, development and application through training on a regular, systematic basis. Psychological training should incorporate methods and techniques which teach you how to interpret what is happening to you and why, how to cope with whatever you encounter, how to make decisions based on relevant cues, and how to persist despite what is happening. In short, you need to learn the cognitive skills and strategies that are necessary for controlling your sport performance. These skills are not concomitant learnings that just happen when playing or competing. They are skills which have to be learned and practiced to enhance your performance.

In the past, coaches and athletes have been able to get away with explaining the deficiencies by using vague psychological jargon about performance or behavior. As an example, saying such things as "he choked," "he couldn't take the pressure," "she's too emotional," do not excuse one from the responsibility of doing something about coping with the situations encountered in competition. In fact, not including coping strategies and skills constitutes a training failure in this day and age. In today's world, each of us is charged with the responsibility for controlling our behavior. We can no longer transfer the responsibility or excuse for behavioral failures to others or to some mysterious factor. It is no longer appropriate for us to talk in psychological terms as though we are knowledgable in psychology if we do not make some effort to become informed and educated in this area. It is unfair to continue attributing shortcomings in performance to psychological factors and not to do something about it. The days of coaching and/or performing through "hope" are no longer appropriate or effective. There are techniques and strategies that enable us to control and to monitor our behavior in sport so we can develop consistent performance and maximize our potential. Only when our athletic weaknesses are minimized do we have a chance of achieving our true potential in performance. Strengths and weaknesses can be classified in behavioral as well as physical terms.

It stands to reason you do not perform correctly all the time; however, you can be taught to analyze your own behavior so that you understand why there was performance inconsistency. You can be taught to work toward more consistent control over your behavior once you learn to analyze it and determine what factors influence it.

In the process of developing skills strategies for teaching control of behavior in sport, situations that are characteristic of specific sports and behaviors that are sport-specific must be understood. It has become increasingly obvious that you have to understand the behavioral demands being placed on you to cope with these demands. You must understand what you are to do! Further you need to have some insight into the possible situations that may occur within your sport. Without this, it is difficult to prepare for what might happen!

Any athlete who plays competitively faces stressful situations and anxious moments hundreds of times over the course of his/her competitive experiences. You do not have to be a professional athlete to experience those anxious moments when your heart starts pounding, your hands get sweaty, and you feel weak in the knees. For many, regardless of how many times they have been in that situation, they still react in the same way. Somehow, experience is not the best teacher in this case!

These moments of anxiety, which can be pure panic in some situations, interfere with performance at every level. Athletes who continue to perform with some degree of consistency, despite their feelings of anxiety, have learned to cope in one way or another. Relatively few of us, however, have been taught skills and strategies that would enable us to cope and maintain some consistency in performance. We have been helped with our physical skills and strategies, but few have attempted to help us with the development of our mental skills.

Many athletes with superior physical capabilities have been systematically eliminated from competitive sports because they could not perform with any consistency. They might perform beautifully in practice but "choke" in competition. Coaches have pulled their hair out over athletes who do things correctly in practice for an entire week and on the first play in a game revert back to old habits! Why do these things happen? Has it happened to you? What can you do to try to prevent these situations from repeating year after year, season after season? What can coaches do to help an athlete who is physically endowed but who does not appear to be able to maintain any consistency in performance? How can we help our own performance to become more consistent?

Many people feel having someone teach psychological skills to athletes infers that the athletes are unstable or have "mental problems." This bias among most coaches and even some athletes is that psychologists are people who provide help to those who are disturbed or maladjusted. They would never consider that "normal" athletes were in need of someone trained in sport psychology. Further, many coaches want only tough-minded athletes who "survive the system" and select that biased group for their teams. They do not want what they think are "head problems." Coaches have eliminated athletes who had all the necessary physical assets because they did not appear to be able to perform with any degree of consistency or because they "choked" in pressure situations. They have never stopped to ask if certain skills could be taught to these athletes which would enable them to use their physical abilities effectively.

Relatively few actively participating athletes are in need of trained psychologists. This leaves a select group of athletes who are generally mentally healthy and stable, but who may be in need of some cognitive skills and strategies for learning how to cope with their own arousal in in competitive situations to produce consistent performance. Cognitive skills are teachable ones and any coach or athlete can learn the techniques and methods of incorporating these skills into the practice and competition routine.

Eastern European countries have been utilizing these techniques with regular success during the last several decades. Almost all coaches in these countries are trained in psychological strategies and techniques and incorporate them into their regular training programs for their athletes. It is reported that USSR athletes devote approximately 75 percent of their final training prior to a competiton to the psychological factors and only practice the physical skills enough to maintain their level at that point. Most coaches in this country are still overloading the "programmer" with instructions as the athletes enter the playing area. Many continue to yell instructions regarding physical skill production and strategies throughout the competition but to no avail. It is obvious that coaches and athletes in North America need to be educated to the psychological considerations that impact on learning and help to maximize performance.

First, it should be emphasized that all successful athletes have discovered a way of coping which works for them to some degree. One can observe athletes who resort to rituals prior to every competition. Everything must be done in a ritualistic manner leading up to the actual competition. These rituals may include special diets, special music, special routines, putting on the necessary equipment and uniform in a special manner, wearing a special piece of apparel or carrying a rabbit's foot. All of these rituals contribute to a known and established procedure to ensure some security in the face of a relatively insecure situation. Increasing the number of "knowns" tends to counter the "unknown," which is the outcome of the competition.

Other athletes may appear to be quite calm, cool, and collected on the exterior, but are a "nervous wreck" internally. In defense of their perceived anxiety, they talk "big" and boast loudly about what they will do to their opponents. When they get into competition, they frequently "choke." Then there are those athletes that appear to be in a "twit" and who display all types of nervous mannerisms, yet go into a competition and manage to perform exceptionally well. There are other "types" who could be described as well. The point is, there are many different behaviors observed among athletes in the final stages before competition.

Athletes need to be helped in understanding why they do certain things in preparation for a competition. Most have no idea why they do what they do. They have never associated what they do with how well or how poorly they play for the most part. In short, they may not know why they follow a set routine. Most have developed these patterns by coincidence. If they happen to have done them and then played fairly well, they associate the routine with playing well, thus repeating the procedure in hopes of playing well again! Because of the way they have established the routine, they do not have much control over how to follow it for performance improvement.

You may think you do not need this mental stuff. You are much like Avis, the Number 2 car rental agency who just "tries harder!" Trying harder is not the solution; in many cases, trying harder creates even greater problems. You may think that "going back to the fundamentals" and practicing longer and harder are the only solutions to decrements in performance. Frequently, longer and harder practices are used as punishment for not performing up to your expectations or to the coach's. Obviously, too much emphasis has been placed on the physical aspects of sport performance without understanding *all* the components of performance.

No one disputes the fact that your state of mind has a lot to do with your performance. Yet almost nothing has been done to identify the emotional and/or mental factors that tend to prevent good performance any more than trying to identify those factors that produce poor performance. Basically, that is all sport psychology for the athlete is: learning how to identify what leads to good performance and what leads to poor performance. This is accomplished by observing and taking notes on your own thoughts and behaviors prior to competition. Once these have been determined, you need to learn cognitive skills and strategies to control the dysfunctional ones so you can bring about the conditions that lead to good performance. This provides a basis for understanding why you perform well or inconsistently. You do not have to say, "I just had a good game," or "I had an off-night," you will be able to analyze why you had a good or bad game.

If you were told that the body and mind do not interact, you would most likely disagree. You could cite examples demonstrating how the interaction occurs such as experiencing fear and having that perception of fear being accompanied by sweating, increased heart rate, altered breathing, feeling of muscular weakness, and nausea. Or, you might remember awaking from some nightmare and discover that you are having heart palpitations, sweating, breathing hard, and so on. There are many more examples of the mind-body integration that could be shared here, however, the point is, in athletic performance we have come to believe the mind and the body should be approached separately. We focus our attention on the physical preparation and hope that the rest falls into place!

The body is a highly complex entity composed of a multitude of different, yet highly integrated, biological systems which promote effective interaction between our internal and external environments. These highly differentiated systems are integrated and monitored by the nervous system. The nervous system is anatomically divided into the central and the peripheral nervous system. The brain and spinal cord compose the central nervous system; the network of nerves connecting the various organs and systems of the body to the central nervous system makes up the peripheral nervous system. Thought and memory are the responsibility of the central nervous system. However, the entire nervous system allows the body to interpret consciously and unconsciously our external and internal environments. Some nerves are specialized for sight, smell, touch, temperature, pain, etc., but the entire nervous system coordinates bodily responses to the environment. In sport and exercise (as in most other environmental responses), a combination of reactions occurs. Some of these reactions are at the conscious level while others may occur at a subconscious level. As an example, if you perceive fear your response may be to escape in some way, either by running away or preparing to "fight" for safety. This is Cannon's "fight or flight" response to fear or threat to one's well being. Once this fear is perceived, other responses occur immediately such as elevated blood pressure, increased blood flow to the muscles and vital organs, decreased blood flow to the digestive system, increased metabolism, and so on. In short, all the bodily systems are geared for optimal function for protection. These responses happen with real fear of your physical or mental well being or with the perception of that threat.

In today's society, with an increasing awareness of an holistic approach to well being, we still separate the mind and body and spirit. If something is wrong with our body, we go see a physician. If something is wrong with our mind, we seek out a psychologist or a psychiatrist. And, if we have trouble with our spirit, we visit the clergy. In sport the coach, but mainly the athlete, is responsible for learning the skills and strategies for mental preparation. Since our muscles do not function unless directed to do so by the mind, it appears that when we learn a sport, we are training our minds. We do not isolate certain body parts and expect them to learn a skill such as throwing or kicking without processing that skill in our mind. We do not perform physical skills in isolation without mental skills. Sport performance must be approached from an holistic perspective to integrate the "thinking with our muscles" necessary to produce potential levels of performance.

Hardly anyone disputes the fact that your mental state has a great deal to do with your physical performance. Despite the meager knowledge available concerning the influence of emotional and mental states on performance, we do know that worry and anxiety about how you will perform can cause a sub-par performance. One of the ways to avoid that is to prepare the "whole" person through holistic coaching and preparation. That is, incorporate physical and mental skills and strategies in practice and performance.

After you develop an awareness of how this relationship affects your performance, you are ready to learn skills and strategies to help you control your worry and anxiety. The remainder of this book will cover the skills of relaxation, concentration, imagery and communication. The strategies included are those for self-talk or self-thoughts and goal setting. Various approaches are included for each of these and specific techniques and exercises are included for learning and practicing these. Teaching cues are presented as well as ways of assessing progress in learning these mental skills and stratagies. You may find these helpful in improving your own performance or the performance of your team. The skills and strategies are relevant to sport situations and are geared to maximizing athletic performance. Attainment of the highest level you can reach within your genetic, physiological and biochemical limits and within your own motivation is the goal.

You will not learn these mental skills and strategies in one or two practices any better than you would learn a physical skill or strategy. You need to understand that it does take time to learn these skills just as it takes time to learn physical skills. Regular practice following a logical progression is necessary to become proficient in executing these skills when you need them. Further, the more you practice them, the more likely you can apply them when the situation demands them. It takes discipline, motivation and regular practices over time to produce results.

Some athletes and coaches may feel it is a waste of time to practice these skills and think that just developing an awareness of the relationship of anxiety and peformance is sufficient. It should be emphasized again and again, you must practice them on a regular basis to attain the skill. Once all the skills are learned, they are incorporated into regular practices and performances without a specific time being set aside for their practice.

During the first two or three weeks there may be little evidence of any positive results or that anything is happening. You must understand that this is a normal response and be motivated to continue to practice. As you begin to acquire the skill, many of the responses are subtle. Most athletes are not aware of them unless they are really "tuned in" to their bodies. At the same time, the practices schedule for mental skills should be short compared to the physical practices. It is important to practice a short period of time on a regular basis. With frequent practice and step by step progressions, you should see some progress within three weeks. If not, be patient and continue practicing. Some individuals need more time for practicing before the results become obvious.

The greatest effect of training to develop mental skills comes after longer periods of practice and application. In short, like most other things, the more you use it appropriately, the better you become! With time, the responses practiced and the skills and strategies learned become automatic. Eventually, this type of behavioral response becomes a way of thinking and perceiving. It becomes a way of responding that is much more effective, more positive, and more conducive to realizing your potential in whatever you pursue. The principles are the same for regulating your arousal and managing your worry about performance whether it be on the athletic field, taking a written examination, public speaking, acting on stage, being interviewed for the job of your life, or whatever. Learning and practicing these skills will last you a lifetime and allow you to enjoy your performance much more at a much higher level than you have previously attained.

Sometimes when we "play over our head" and experience that peak performance we describe it as being in an " altered state of awareness or consciousness." It is though we are in a "trance" or in another state. It is ironic that this state is referred to as an "altered state" when it occurs! In point of fact, perhaps this is the way we should be responding to these situations all the time. Getting "our act together" happens so infrequently that we are amazed when it happens and are at a loss to explain why it does occur. With practice and development of a greater awareness of how you respond to situations, you can make it a "regular state" rather than an "altered state." If you are to reach your potential level of performance, you must begin to incorporate mental training in your daily preparation.

2

WORRY AND ANXIETY ABOUT PERFORMANCE

Worrying about how you are going to perform leads to becoming anxious about your performance. Anxiety is manifested both in physical or somatic ways and in cognitive or mental ways. This sequence occurs when you worry about anything whether it be taking an exam, making a speech, meeting important people, having an interview for a job, or playing in the most important athletic competition you've ever faced. The body has only a limited number of ways to show when you are worried and concerned. These responses are similar in all situations even though the cause may be quite different. We do not worry just in our heads, our whole body worries. As a result, anytime we worry, we experience some reaction in our body as well as in our mental state. This fact is a critical one regarding performance.

Whenever we worry and become anxious we experience disruption and dysfunction to some degree. The more worried we become, the more anxiety we experience and the greater the degree of disruption of performance. In sport we call this "choking" or being "uptight." Mental errors as well as tactical and execution errors occur. Our bodies provide us with a great number of warnings that we are "getting out of control." Some of the immediate physical or somatic cues are: palpitations of the heart, muscle tension, sense of fatigue, irritability, cotton mouth, cold, clammy hands and feet, butterflies in the stomach, the desire to urinate, visual distortion, trembling and twitches in muscles, flushed face, voice distortion, nausea and vomiting, diarrhea, hyperventilation, increased heart rate, blood pressure and respiratory rate. Some of the cognitive cues or warnings are: sense of confusion, forgetting details, inability to concentrate, resorting to old habits and inability to make decisions. Obviously, if one had all these symptoms at once, complete dysfunction would occur.

Most of us have some combination of these when we get nervous, scared and worried about not performing well on the task we face. Individuals differ in how much their performance is affected, therefore, it is essential to identify the responses you associate with anxiety and to determine how they influence your performance.

I Have Seen the Enemy and It Is I

Each time you perform, whether it be in practice or during a competition, you have certain expectations and hopes about how that performance will be. If your performance falls short of your expectancies, then you generally begin to worry. Expectations are generated by past performance and feedback. Past perfomances shape the expectations of future performances. In fact, past performance is the best predictor of expected future performance. This is why you may become more anxious in a performance following one where you did not play up to your usual level. You begin to worry that you may have another poor performance.

For worry to take place, you will have to perceive differences between what you hope for, what is actually happening, and what you expect to happen. You have to be able to read your cognitive (mental) and somatic (body) cues and interpret them in the correct manner. Since we have only a limited number of ways to respond to stimulation, whether it be induced cognitively or somatically, it is essential to interpret these responses properly. To explain further, regardless of whether you are exercising, being frightened to death, worried about failing an exam, experiencing a strong emotion such as love, anger, or exhilaration, your response will follow a similar pattern. This response involves an elevated heart rate, change in the respiratory pattern, sweating, elevated blood pressure, possibly trembling, flushed skin, voice distortion, accompanied sometimes by inability to concentrate or to remember details, and a sense of confusion. Only you can interpret the cues and determine the cause! In fact, if you were wired up to equipment that would measure all of these variables and were located out of our sight where we could only read your responses, we would not know what was causing them. Only you could tell us!

Because our bodies can only respond in this limited fashion to whatever we encounter that is arousing, it is essential that each of us learns to read and interpret our own cues accurately. Many athletes associate the cognitive and somatic manifestations of worry and anxiety about their performance as being "psyched up" and ready for competition. You need to learn how to distinguish your response of worry from those caused by being excited and ready for the challenge of competition. The distinction between these two has sometimes been referred to as "good arousal" and "bad arousal." The bad arousal is that generated by worry and fear about your performance while the good arousal is produced by the excitement and feelings of "let me get at them." Only you can know what causes your arousal. The remaining chapters of this book will help you learn how to read your own cues to determine your optimal performance state and to regulate your arousal so you do not let it get out of control and interfere with your performance.

Worry that produces anxiety is almost always dysfunctional and disruptive to your performance. It is worry about fear of failure or not performing up to your expectations that causes you to "blank out on an exam." The same thing will cause you to "blow your lines on stage" or even forget the name of someone you have known for years when you begin to introduce them in a social situation that may be an anxious one for you. The task you have before you is to learn how to interpret these responses and learn to regulate them to the extent that you do not become dysfunctional. In short, the effects produced by anxiety and worry never facilitate good performance. Anxiety disrupts cognitive control and "jams the programmer" so you do not perform at your potential level.

Fortunately, worry does not begin at the point where you perceive a difference between your expectancies and you perception of the situation. As a result, you have time to begin to regulate the response to keep it under control. The uncertainty that exists regarding the outcome of performance contributes to worry and anxiety as well. Not knowing what the outcome will be and being afraid that it will not be what you wish, threatens your sense of well-being. In essence, it is the "fight or flight" response which prepares you for running away or staying to face it. Unfortunately, we have difficulty separating out what may be a threat to our physical well-being from a threat to our mental well-being. For the most part, there is no actual threat to our physical well-being, only to our self-esteem and mental well-being. Nevertheless, the "fight or flight" is the same.

When a threat to our well-being exists our mind begins to

play tricks with us. Just remember back to when you listened to a ghost story, how afraid you got and how you imagined all sorts of strange sounds and noises when you went to bed that night. The same sort of "run-away," imaginative thoughts are activated when you begin to worry about your sport performance. Later in this book you will read about self-thoughts and self-talk and about imagery or the use of your imagination. While these strategies can make a positive contribution to controlling your worry and anxiety, they can also make it worse. Once you begin to worry about the bad things that might happen to make you look foolish during your performance, your self-thoughts begin to create dysfunction. Accompanying the negative thoughts are usually mental pictures of your anticipated disaster. Good ol' Charlie Brown is a classic example of this type of mental processing. He is forever talking himself out of a good game by reliving yesterday's disaster and worrying about all the ways he can make a fool out of himself in today's game. Charlie is always in constant turmoil and will never be able to perform as he would like to as long as he has all these negative thoughts and images about how he will play.

Most of us follow a general process when we try to solve situations perceived as problematic. When facing a problem, it is normal to feel more aroused, to experience some anxiety and to try to analyze the situation based on our previous experience and the clues we can pick up in the present situation. From there, we try to get our act together by constructing mental and emotional defenses against the threat to our self-esteem. However, it is after this point that most of us track-off in the wrong direction. Instead of using all the information in a constructive and coping manner, we let the worry lead us to pondering when we cannot find a ready solution. Contemplating the problem becomes our downfall if we cannot devise some way to resolve our concern. This sequence of mental processing leads us to greater stress which, in turn creates more dysfunction in our performance. This is the process called "choking" in sport.

As mentioned earlier, we have two possible responses to the initial worry: we can either direct it toward a productive end and cope with the situation or we can worry in circles and in an unproductive manner and generate even greater anxiety. The two possible outcomes are presented in Figure 1.

The unproductive option which most of us follow, unless we learn skills and strategies to cope, results in a persistent preoccupation of our mind. We speculate, rehash, project the worst with

FIGURE 1. TWO POSSIBLE RESPONSE PATTERNS TO INITIAL WORRY ABOUT PERFORMANCE

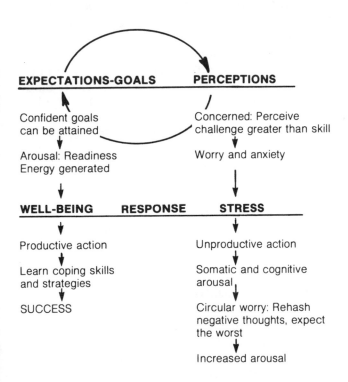

EXPECTATIONS-GOALS   **PERCEPTIONS**

Confident goals   Concerned: Perceive
can be attained   challenge greater than skill

Arousal: Readiness   Worry and anxiety
Energy generated

WELL-BEING   RESPONSE   STRESS

Productive action   Unproductive action

Learn coping skills   Somatic and cognitive
and strategies   arousal

SUCCESS   Circular worry: Rehash
                             negative thoughts, expect
                             the worst

                             Increased arousal

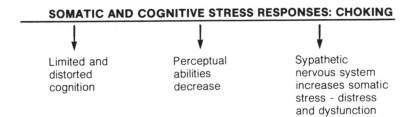

SOMATIC AND COGNITIVE STRESS RESPONSES: CHOKING

Limited and   Perceptual   Sypathetic
distorted   abilities   nervous system
cognition   decrease   increases somatic
                                         stress - distress
                                         and dysfunction

Adapted from Barbara Brown, SUPERMIND (New York: Harper & Row, 1980) negative thoughts and images about what the outcome might be. We continue this preoccupation, combining and re-combining all possible disastrous outcomes. It becomes a self-defeating and a destructive cycle of worry. We become so preoccupied with the impending disaster that we cannot possibly understand why we fail to cope with the problem.

The sixty-four thousand dollar question is, where can you interrupt the events to prevent disruption and dysfunction of performance? It appears that you must intervene at the worry stage while you can still direct your attention to eliminating the problem or learn to regulate your arousal resulting from the worry long enough to discover a solution or eliminate the problem. Once you switch to the preoccupation stage your attention usually switches as well to focusing on your internal distress caused by the problem rather than focusing on a solution. So, what you must do is learn mental skills and strategies to regulate your arousal so you can resolve the problem in a constructive manner. The remainder of the book is devoted to understanding and learning how to regulate your arousal so that you can maximize your performance in every situation in sport.

Understanding the Terminology

To clarify (or to further add to the confusion), it is necessary to discuss some of the terms that are frequently used in describing the mind/body response to perceived threat. Most of the psychological literature uses the term *arousal* which refers to the intensity of the response. This can vary from deep sleep to intense excitement. Much of the literature on motivation is related to the degree of arousal present in the situation. The original work in this area concluded that the more aroused one was, the more motivated. Discussion which follows later in this chapter should clarify that issue, particularly regarding good and bad arousal.

Anxiety is generally considered to be a combination of the cognitive and somatic manifestations of perceived emotional or physical threat. It has been further divided into several subcatagories. Trait anxiety is one's predisposition to perceive certain stimuli as threatening. Individuals with high trait anxiety levels are generally more "hyper" than those with lower levels. They tend to exhibit a chronically higher level of arousal in all situations. State anxiety is the situation-specific anxiety state. That is, how anxious are you at this point in time as opposed to how anxious are you in general? State anxiety is the current or existing emotional state and refers to the response along two dimensions, intensity and direction. These are aroused by the perception of danger, fear of failure and worry or threat to self-esteem in a particular situation. State anxiety is most relevant to competitive sport situations. More about that later.

State anxiety has been further divided into two additional dimensions. The somatic or bodily anxiety is distinguished from the cognitive or mental anxiety. Some individuals tend to display much more of one of these dimensions than another. There are athletes who exhibit a tremendous amount of physical or bodily anxiety but who are calm, cool and collected mentally. Conversely, there are athletes who appear physically collected and under control who are cognitively confused, distracted, and unable to concentrate. In general, the research on athletes suggests that most athletes experience a great deal of somatic anxiety prior to a competition. This dissipates fairly quickly once action begins. In fact, this manifestation may be a positive one as it reflects the readiness and arousal the athlete has generated. On the other hand, if the cognitive level is high, this might suggest the athlete is too aroused to concentrate and prepare for the competition. High somatic arousal suggests that the focus is on the upcoming competition; just thinking about it generates considerable somatic arousal. Helping the athletes determine what is causing the arousal and how to interpret what is happening will assist in teaching them how to use this energy to their advantage rather than worrying about it.

The use of the term stress as a cause or response of threat has been avoided until recently. Hans Selye, a pioneer in stress research, defined it as, "the nonspecific response of the body to any demand made upon it." Early on he pointed out that the response to both good stress (eustress) or bad stress (distress) was manifested in the same way physiologically. The response to good arousal or bad arousal is manifested in a similar fashion. The difference may be that which is highlighted in Figure 1, that is, good stress or confident, readiness arousal does not lead to circular worry and dysfunction.

Stress has frequently been the term used to describe the external condition that leads to arousal. As an example, we speak of competitive stress, of heat stress, or of exercise stress, meaning that it is the "cause" of the arousal. More recently, however, stress has become a term that describes the condition rather than the cause when discussing behavioral response.

FIGURE 2 CHECKLIST FOR DETERMINING RELATIONSHIP OF RESPONSE AND PERFORMANCE

WHEN IT OCCURS

RESPONSE	PRACTICE	PRE-COMPETITION	COMPETITION	EVALUATION OF PLAY
Heart Palpitations	_____	_____	_____	_____
Muscle tensions	_____	_____	_____	_____
Feeling of fatigue	_____	_____	_____	_____
Cotton mouth	_____	_____	_____	_____
Clammy hands and feet	_____	_____	_____	_____
Butterflies in stomach	_____	_____	_____	_____
Desire to urinate	_____	_____	_____	_____
Visual distortion	_____	_____	_____	_____
Nasea	_____	_____	_____	_____
Vomiting	_____	_____	_____	_____
Diarrhea	_____	_____	_____	_____
Trembling and twitching muscles	_____	_____	_____	_____
Hyperventilation	_____	_____	_____	_____
Increased heart rate	_____	_____	_____	_____
Increased respiratory rate	_____	_____	_____	_____
Yawning	_____	_____	_____	_____
Voice distortion	_____	_____	_____	_____
Flushed skin	_____	_____	_____	_____
Irritability	_____	_____	_____	_____
Sense of confusion	_____	_____	_____	_____
Forgetting details	_____	_____	_____	_____
Inability to concentrate	_____	_____	_____	_____
Inability to make decisions	_____	_____	_____	_____
Resorting to old habits	_____	_____	_____	_____

For the purposes of this book, many of the terms may be used interchangeably. What we are talking about is any interruption or distraction that may interfere with performance. The following listing in Figure 2 will provide you with disruptions and observations that athletes have experienced prior to performance. Obviously, you will not have experienced them all at once or you may not have experienced very many of them in the past. Use this listing as your guide to becoming more aware and in tune with your body so that you can begin to associate these feelings with the type of performance that you have. Making these associations will help you learn what feelings are associated with bad performances. Once you establish the pattern, you will be in a position to set the stage for having the type of performance you would like to have each time!

Arousal and Performance Relationships

Combining the experiences of athletes and the research that has been conducted to this point in time, a pattern of arousal and performance has been documented. It is now obvious that the over used approach of "winning one for the Gipper" speech in the locker room is not necessarily the best way to generate arousal to maximize performance! Strategies of degrading, berating, insulting, humiliating, aggressive verbal or physical approaches, or playing on someone's sympathy do not work in most situations either. Learning to tune into your own body, to become aware of your own responses and to assume responsibility for controlling them works much better in all situations. It provides you with a sense of power and control that reinforces self-confidence and security in your own ability to handle whatever occurs.

Relatively little is known about "psyching-up" strategies that actually work. Most people are of the opinion that an athlete is not "ready" to perform unless he/she is excited, hyperactive and foaming at the mouth! Most coaches think that an athlete is not motivated and ready to play unless some of these observations can be made. If you have prepared well both physically and mentally and are confident of your ability to deal with the upcoming situation, you do not need to be all "psyched" by some external means to get ready to perform. Obviously, we all need a certain level of arousal to get the job done. This amount of arousal is highly individualized; some of us need much more than others to perform at the same level. Our job is to learn just what the right level is to maximize our potential.

Recent studies and self-reports from elite athletes suggest that most all athletes experience high levels of pre-competitive somatic anxiety with some experiencing extremely high levels. The pattern is one of increasing physical manifestations of anxiety. Many of these athletes, despite these high levels of anxiety, perform exceptionally well and consistently close to their potential. As a result of these findings, one has to conclude that it is not the absence of anxiety per se that leads to consistent superior performance. Instead, it appears that the determining factor is how the athlete perceives this increasing manifestation of anxiety about the upcoming performance and how he or she will channel that arousal and energy that is being generated. Becoming more aware of what your responses are and the conditions under which they occur can help you to accept this as part of your readiness for consistently good performances.

Pre-competitive anxiety among the elite athletes is manifested physically, as indicated earlier. There appears to be a virtual absence of cognitive manifestations of anxiety. This may be the significant factor that separates the consistently superior performer from those who fluctuate a great deal in their performances. In the absence of cognitive disruption, elite athletes can focus and direct (or channel) the arousal and energy they are experiencing in a constructive direction. In other words, you must learn to focus on the upcoming performance, disregarding the physical manifestations in such a way that you do not associate them with anything other than "this is the way I feel when I perform at my best." All the skills and strategies that follow later in this book will assist you in learning to accomplish that. Incorporating these skills in both your practices and performances, accompanied by practice sessions and performances in environments that increase your arousal and anxiety, will assist you in learning to cope with any situation. You need to learn how to "harness" all that energy being generated via your arousal system and apply it to the upcoming performance. Learn to have it work for you instead of interfering with your performance. Learning to "switch channels" will be discussed in a later section; this skill is essential to applying your energy where it will help rather than hinder you.

Keep in mind that beyond a certain level of competition, it is not the physical but the mental skills that an athlete brings to the competition that count the most. You are not a "born winner" or a "born loser"; you learn to be whatever you are. As a result, you can learn other behaviors to replace the undesirable ones. Once you learn to distinguish between "psyching up" and "psyching out," you are well on your way! "Psyching out" is caused by worry and anxiety which lead to over arousal. In short, it leads to choking! You have to learn what your optimal arousal is to maximize your performance.

Your Optimal Level of Arousal for Superior Performance

There exists an optimal level of arousal for optimal performance for each of us. This may differ from one individual to another, therefore, it is necessary to determine your own optimal level. If your level is too low, you may not perform the task or skill as well as you might because you will not be motivated sufficiently. This relationship was the one that directed the efforts of psychologists toward associating arousal levels with motivation. However, this relationship of more arousal equals more motivation only applies to the lower end of the arousal scale. Most of the classic upsets in sport occur because of this. If the opponent(s) are perceived to be much less able than you or your team, there is a tendency to think you can win easily. As a result, you are not aroused sufficiently to perform at the level that may be needed to experience success. Then, when you discover that you will have to become more effective, that your opponent(s) are much better than you expected, you have difficulty "re-programming" your efforts. The solution is to be able to face each and every challenge with your arousal under control. This means that you need to identify your optimal level and begin each event with that level. If you let your arousal get out of hand and go beyond the optimal level, you will have problems as well. These problems are more difficult to control. However, without some regulation of your arousal level, you will experience disruption and dysfunction. Rapid deterioration will occur; the greater the arousal, the greater the deterioration of your performance. Figure 3 shows that relationship.

FIGURE 3 - THE AROUSAL — PERFORMANCE RELATIONSHIP

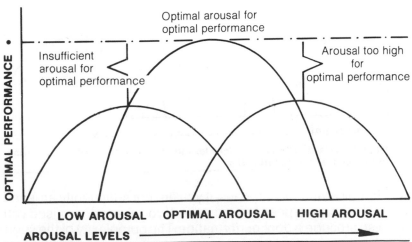

Your required level of arousal is also related to the degree of complexity of the task and the length of time necessary to execute that task. For example, as a lineman on a football team, you can probably get by with a higher level of arousal and still accomplish your task easier than if you were a receiver, kicker, or quarterback. This relationship of task difficulty and the level of arousal is due to the fact that gross motor tasks that are accomplished in a short period of time are less affected by high levels of arousal than precise tasks that require concentration, reading relevant cues, and decision making. The relationship of task difficulty and arousal is shown in Figure 4.

FIGURE 4 - RELATIONSHIP OF COMPLEXITY OF TASK AND AROUSAL.

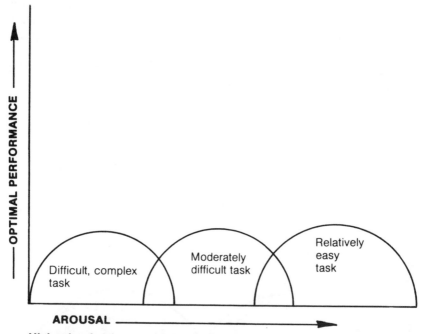

Higher levels of arousal interfere less in simple gross motor skills than in complex and difficult tasks.

For all practical purposes, if you are not sufficiently aroused you will produce a poor performance. If you are over aroused you will also produce a poor performance. The complexity of the sport or position that you play within a sport and the amount of time required to execute the task will influence the performance as well. The more precise and complex the task, the greater the disruption to the performance when over aroused. What you need to do is find a balance between under and over arousal or your *optimal level.*

Mihaly Csikszentmihalyi, author of BEYOND BOREDOM AND ANXIETY, has developed a concept that applies to finding this balance for peak performance. He suggests that the challenge must be equal to the skill level to experience "flow" or the feeling that everything is going just right in your performance. Anytime you perceive that the challenge of your opponent or of playing as you would like is beyond your skill level, you experience worry and anxiety. On the other hand, when your skills are much greater than the perceived challenge, you become bored and do not "rise to the occasion." The optimal level or the desired balance is when your skills and capabilities are equal to the challenge you face. This can be controlled to some degree by the opponents that you select, however, that is not always possible. Goal setting within your overall plan of increasing your skills and capabilities will help to attain a state of flow or balance. Goal setting will be discussed at length later in the book.

See FIGURE 5 for the relationship of your perceptions of your abilities and the challenge you face. As indicated in the figure, when the ratio is in balance, you experience FLOW or a sense of everything going perfectly. Everything you do works! On the other hand, when the ratio is disproportionate in either direction your performance suffers. This is related to the optimal arousal concept. When your ability exceeds the challenge you do not generate sufficient arousal and become bored. If this state continues, you will not be able to "get your game going" and will become anxious with the inability to play as you would like or have in the past. This is the general pattern of the classic upsets in sport. That is, you fail to see the upcoming competition as a challenge. This results in your not "rising to the occasion" by getting aroused sufficiently to perform well.

If the perception of the challenge you face is much greater than the perception of your ability you will begin to worry. This leads to over arousal and on to anxiety which, in turn, leads to dysfunction and a poor performance. As you can see, the ideal performance state is when your skills and abilities are approximately equal to the challenge. Setting short-term goals on a regular basis to improve skills and abilities will increase your capabilities. Beyond that, seeking opponents who provide the proper ratio of challenge to your skill will set the stage for peak performance on a regular basis.

If you can remember a time when you felt that you played

FIGURE 5 — THE CONCEPT OF LOW: WHEN PERCEPTION OF ABILITY IS EQUAL TO THE PERCEIVED CHALLENGE

(If the ratio is not balanced, worry, boredom and anxiety result, depending on whether challenge exceeds ability or ability exceeds challenge.)
Adapted from M. Csikszentmihalyi, BEYOND BOREDOM AND ANXIETY (San Francisco: Jossey-Bass Publishers, 1975)

"over your head, that everything flowed," you may remember that you felt confident and ready for the challenge. There was no worry or anxiety about how you might perform. In short, your skills and capabilities were equal to the challenge you faced in your athletic competition. You can learn to "set the stage" for flow by regulating your awareness in the situation so it is compatible with flow. That is, learn to become aware but not aware of your awareness! Think about that: *Aware but not aware of your awareness.* This means that you need to be focused on what you are doing in a very passive manner, just let it happen without trying to "make it happen!" If you have experienced a time when everything went "just right," you probably remember that it felt effortless, that you could do nothing wrong, that you did the right thing at the right time without even thinking about it! That is the ideal performance state. Just learn to tune into your body so you can have total integration with all the physical and mental components of the performance synchronized. There is no evidence of past thoughts or worries, you feel confident and completely in control. You can execute your physical skills without being aware of thinking about them at all. You are totally engulfed in the here and now with a sense of effortlessness in whatever you do. You will experience the feeling of your skills and assignments being executed automatically, almost without your interfering with the process. And, you'll experience more fun and enjoyment than ever before as you begin to perform with consistency as you improve in all your efforts. This will be a regular part of your participation and involvement once you learn what your optimal level of arousal is and how you can tune in to it for every practice or competition.

Sources of Worry and Anxiety

Worry and anxiety are almost always self-produced! Our perception of the situation creates most of our problems, however, anxiety is produced by many factors.

Having unrealistic beliefs about your performance, that is, thinking that you will perform poorly can cause anxiety. It is not the competitive situation per se that causes it. You can set the stage for a poor performance by processing negative self-thoughts which distort the situation you are about to face.

Believing in "worry" and thinking that you are supposed to be nervous is another source of anxiety. Some athletes do not feel they are "psyched" and ready to play unless they experience all types of physical and mental manifestations of anxiety.

Having experienced a sub-standard performance during your last competition is a source of anxiety as well. If you allow yourself to become preoccupied with feelings of past disasters and worries about impending ones, you are bound to become more anxious! This leads to the circular, unproductive attempt to find a solution for relieving your stress.

Believing that your self-worth as an individual is dependent upon your athletic performance can produce a tremendous amount of anxiety. It is this situation that generates the threat to your self-esteem which in turn leads to physical and mental responses that interfere with your performance.

Obviously, it is highly unlikely that anyone can eliminate anxiety completely; there are just too many realistic pressures in athletic competition. However, every athlete can minimize the frequency and the intensity of the anxiety experienced through learning mental and physical skills and stategies. Sources and symptoms of anxiety are countered by approaching performance from a holistic perspective. Physically, athletes can be taught to relax their bodily tensions. Mentally they can learn to restructure thoughts and images that are counterproductive to good performance. They can increase their ability to concentrate, to use imagery and to communicate. You can learn these skills as well if you will practice them systematically and regularly. This type of control *will not* take the edge off your competitiveness. Instead, it will facilitate greater concentration and intensity and prevent interference of both internal and external distractions to your performance. Every competition should be a peak performance!

Accounting for Individual Differences

Fortunately, we are not all alike! Just as each of us has our own optimal level of arousal, each of us has a nervous system that may be unique with regard to how it responds to stimulation. People do differ in speed of response in excitation and inhibition of stimuli. If you are one who has difficulty getting up in the morning you can appreciate this difference. If you need to have several alarm clocks, backed up by someone who will come and physically shake you in order to awaken you and get you on your feet, you are quite different from individuals who can "program" themselves to awaken at whatever time they desire without an alarm. Further, you may need a cold shower, several cups of coffee and a couple of hours of sensory input before your nervous system begins to function at the right speed. Numerous studies have examined the differences between the "larks" or morning people and the "owls" or night people. There are differences that have relevance for sport performance and exercise. If you perform best in the morning and find that late afternoons and evenings do not provide ideal working conditions, you would be classified as a lark. You probably have little difficulty getting up in the morning and wake up ready to go! On the other hand, if you find that you do not begin to function before noon and that your productivity is much greater in the afternoon and evening, you would be considered an owl. If you are a lark, you may find that exercise and sport performance is best in the earlier part of the day. If you are an owl, then you would have more difficulty performing early in the morning. Each can adjust to the situation, however, competitive sport events do not always take these differences into consideration. As a result, you may have to adjust your sleeping schedule as part of your preparation.

These generalized differences have been examined within Eysenckian theory as well. Hans Eysenck says there is a biological difference between individuals with regard to critical arousal. Extroverts generate excitatory potentials slowly and produce a weak stimulus. As a result, it takes more input to generate a response. Introverts, on the other hand, generate excitatory potential quickly and produce a strong stimulus. They require less sensory input to get aroused or to respond.

It has been said that athletes are "stimulus-seeking extroverts." That is, they seek out situations where there is a lot of action: speed, sound, color, and all types of sensory input. They require more to get aroused. Extroverts have a much higher threshold for arousal than introverts. They perform much better in environments where more stimulation is available; they can perform in situations where higher arousal states are expected. As a result, it is not surprising to find that the team sport athletic population tends to be categorized as extroverts. In addition, they have higher tolerance to pain. They seek out situations which produce high arousal: sport, exercise, risk-taking pursuits, etc. They have better gross motor movements than fine ones and tend to stress speed over accuracy. Extroverts express a need for variations on the theme to keep them aroused to prevent boredom from repetition. In most ways, competitive sport provides the environment that is compatible with their behavioral demands and needs.

Introverts are just the opposite of the extroverts in most of their behavioral needs and optimal performance situations. They have a lower arousal threshold and perform better under conditions producing low arousal. They are better at precise, fine motor skills and skills that are repetitious since they have better concentration and longer attention spans than the extroverts. They condition to performing tasks more easily than extroverts due to their concentration and tolerance of repetitious actions. They stress accuracy over speed. They also have a low tolerance to pain but since they condition well, they can condition to the pain experienced in distance track events. As a result, it is not surprising to find a greater proportion of distance runners and swimmers tending toward introversion as opposed to extroversion.

Obviously, there are advantages and disadvantages in being one extreme or the other. Learning more about where you fall along this continuum from introversion to extroversion will help you establish more appropriate practice schedules and goals. It will also help you understand why you might get bored with certain types of practices and drills, why you like or dislike certain types of sports, and why you tend to do certain types of tasks better than other types. Falling toward one end of the continuum or the other has relatively little to do with athleticism per se. It is not related to the natural athletic ability and talent that you have nor to your physical makeup. However, it may help explain why you might have the physical components necessary for a particular sport and the talent to play it but just not be "turned on" to the sport because it does not seem to be compatible with your makeup. Competitive team sports are learned in an environment that is much more compatible with extroversion. It is possible that potentially talented introverts who might have become superior performers under the right conditions have been systematically eliminated from the team sports environment. In other words, only the tough-minded extroverts seek out these environments and can tolerate the behavioral demands since they require so much more stimulation to become aroused. Consequently, they can tolerate competitive situations that generate arousal to a greater extent before their performance drops due to distraction and interference.

Another individual difference that must be accounted for is the type of warmup you require for your best performance. This may well be related to the degree of arousal needed for the ideal performance state. Some athletes need very little warmup. In fact, too much is detrimental to their performance. On the other hand, many other athletes require a great deal more stretching and sport-specific warmup before they are ready for their peak performance. You must determine this for yourself as well and assume the responsibility for warming up in such a manner that you have set the stage for maximizing your potential performance. If you find your needs differ from those of most of your teammates and you feel you need to individualize your warmup, communicate this to the coach. You will have to become aware of how you warmup and how you play in order to determine what approach produces the best performance. Keeping a notebook of the procedures you follow and the resulting performance is the ideal way to determine the relationship of what you do and how you perform.

What You Can Expect When You Identify Your Optimal Level of Arousal

Athletes who experience superior performances consistently report that they feel they can do anything during their performance. They express these feelings and emotions with terms such as, "pumped up," "wired" or "psyched." Positive feelings and emotions create tremendous energy and trigger the optimal level of arousal when you learn how to produce and regulate them. When you focus on the challenge of the situation (as opposed to the pressure), your energy will be utilized in a positive manner rather than in a manner that becomes detrimental to your performance.

Focusing on your own internal state and your own feelings and emotions, as a function of your ideal performance state, emphasizes the fact that your are a conscious participant in regulating your arousal. As a conscious participant, you develop the capacity and ability to feel and to experience what is going on in your body. To understand this, and to experience this cognitively and physically in a fine-tuned, integrated manner, will give you a sense of power and control beyond that which you have probably experienced up to this point.When you develop the confidence to control and direct this energy in a constructive manner, your involvement will become much more positive and satisfying. The arousal you experience will be viewed as pleasant and positive rather than unpleasant and negative to your performance. The right kind of feelings, thoughts, and emotional states produce the optimal level of arousal. Research and self-reports from athletes clearly demonstrate that the same levels of activation and arousal generated by feelings of fear, anger, aggression, frustration, and worry have entirely different performance consequences than comparable arousal levels that are generated by challenge, excitement, exhilaration, a sense of power and control, and readiness to "get at them." Instead of the "fight or flight" response, generate a challenge response! Positive attitudes, feelings of confidence, calmness, effortlessness, power and control generate high energy and arousal that facilitate consistently high performance and allow you to maximize your talent and skill. These capabilities do not just happen, they evolve as a result of strong dedication and commitment to discovery and maintenance of your optimal level of performance. Only you can determine that because only you can become aware of all you experience mentally and physically as you practice and perform in competitive sports. In order to improve, you must get to know your responses and begin to associate them with your performance. The remaining chapters in this book will assist you in accomplishing that goal.

3

LEARNING TO HANG LOOSE

You cannot be uptight and hang loose at the same time! What do we mean when we say someone is uptight? Are they tense? What do we mean by tension? What causes it? Is it bad? How do we know when we are too tense?

If a muscle is tense, it is contracted and in use. Even the slightest mental or bodily activity includes the contracting of some muscles. Take inventory of your muscle activity at this moment. How many and which of your muscles are tense, that is, in use? Are you using muscles other than those necessary to sit and read this? Are your legs crossed? Are you wiggling or kicking your foot? Are you pulling on your hair, or doing things with your hands that have nothing to do with reading? Are you sitting stiffly? Do you have a wrinkled brow or a frown? What about the muscles in your shoulders and neck? Which muscle groups are you using that have nothing to do with reading? Can't you let them go a little bit more? If the answer to any of these questions is "yes," you are not as relaxed as you might be. You have muscles working over time. These relatively small tensions constantly tighten muscles all day long, building up pressures and irritabilities that lead to mistakes, fatigue and other difficulties.

How much unnecessary tension do you have in your muscles? How do you know when you are too tense? Edmund Jacobson, who developed scientific neuromuscular relaxation (which we will discuss later), got interested in relaxation when he was studying the "nervous start." The nervous start is that reaction we have to the unexpected "boo" or to a strange noise. Early in his research Jacobson discovered the more tense and nervous the person appeared to be, the greater the nervous start. We can provide examples of that in terms of an unexpected noise. If it is during the day and you are in a familiar place, the reaction is not so great. On the other hand, if it is dark and stormy and you are in a strange house, the lights have just gone out and you hear an unexpected noise, the "nervous start" reaction is much, much greater. The more anxiety you feel, the greater the response to incoming stimuli. In short, you are already aroused to a high level and additional input pushes it even higher.

Another way to test this relationship is to sit with the lower leg swinging free without support in much the same way as you would have it when the physician is checking your patellar reflex. Tap the patellar tendon when the leg is relaxed and notice the response. Now tap the tendon when you tighten your thigh muscles and observe the difference. The more tension you have in your muscles, the greater the response.

If you are the type that, just before you drop off to sleep, your muscles "jump" as though you have just had 250 volts of electricity put through your body, you have too much tension. Theoretically, you should never have that much tension in your body. This "jerk" response is caused by the muscles that flex "letting go" or relaxing before the extensors. The extensors, in turn, take up the slack produced by the flexors letting go.

Muscle tissue works in only one direction, it can only pull which it does by shortening and thickening itself. Like a string or rope, it can only apply power in one direction. Consequently, the voluntary muscles in all animals must be arranged in pairs, one muscle to "hee" and the other to "haw." When the biceps pull and shorten, the forearm bends; when the triceps in the back of the upper arm shorten, the forearm straightens again. When the forearm is held somewhere in between, both muscles of the pair must pull against each other to produce the proper amount of tension. When a muscle tightens in your body, its opposite of the pair sets up a counter tension to hold that segment of the body in place. This double pull can build up formidable heights of tension over much of the body yet remain unidentified by most people. When a muscle works full time without rest, pain and soreness result. A classic example of this is tension headaches; the muscles in the back of the head and neck are actually sore to the touch. The double pull of muscles also explains why you can literally become scared stiff, frozen with fear, and why you can become rigid with anger. Stage fright, being unable to speak, shooting air balls, blowing a short putt, passing with too much force, or overhitting a tennis ball, are also caused by too much muscular tension.

The principle of the double pull has great significance for athletes. When you watch athletes who move effortlessly, they are using the proper form. The proper form involves using just the right amount of tension necessary to do the skill, to move the body in the most efficient manner with the least amount of energy. Too much muscular tension interferes with execution of the skill. Just think how being afraid of water affects the beginning swimmer; some beginners are absolutely rigid with too much tension. This tension is not produced by the effort to swim but by the mental perception of fear.

This additional and unnecessary muscular tension has been termed "bracing;" the muscles are braced and set for action which seldom occurs. If you are a passenger in a car and you find yourself pushing down on the floor when you think the driver should be braking, that is bracing. Or, a "white knuckle flight" when you are gripping the arms of the seat is bracing. Too much effort in passing a ball to a teammate, in hitting a golf ball, in gripping the steering wheel too hard, are all signs of bracing. Too much tension or bracing can result from physiological input such as pain. It can also result from perceptual or mental input. This is, what you perceive or observe in the environment can create anxiety and produce tension. Cognitive input from your memories, from imagination, from expecting the worst, and other thoughts can produce too much tension as well.

When a muscle is tense, it is contracted or shortened. This contraction involves nerves as well. About half of the nerves in the body are used to alert the muscles or carry the message to the brain. The activity of the nerves, which is electrical in nature, moves along the muscle like a wave with a rapid discharge rate. When this rate increases greatly, there is a high nerve tension and the muscle can become rigid. Our problem, however, is that human nerve-circuits have no automatic regulators. There are no signals to alert you to too much tension. Some individuals unconsciously hold their nerve potential constantly at super high levels. With time, this chronic overcharging can produce many harmful side effects. However, overcharging in an anxiety producing situation such as competitive sport can produce some undesirable results. Choking is probably the best example!

Excess nervous tension is accompanied by excessive muscular tension even when it is triggered mentally. If we can learn to feel our muscular tensions and become sensitive enough to regulate them, we should be able to prevent overcharging and reduce our tension. Nature has provided us with a "built-in tran-quilizer" which we must learn how to use. We can learn to relax, to control our muscular tension without relying on external means.

What Is Relaxation?

Relaxation means letting go and doing absolutely nothing with your muscles. Although the muscles cannot be switched off completely, they can be brought down nicely to an idling speed. This occurs when we drop off to sleep in the process of gradually letting our muscles slip into neutral. Relaxation is the opposite of movement. It is marked by a reduction or complete absence of muscular activity in the voluntary muscles. The reduction or absence of muscular activity in the voluntary muscles is accompanied by a reduction in the involuntary muscles as well. Without the least attention on our part, the heart, circulatory, and breathing muscles continue working, albeit at a much slower pace. Digestion, nutrition, heat formation and other regulatory functions continue as well. Relaxation is a neuromuscular accomplishment which results in a reduction of tension in the skeletal musculature. Even one's so-called normal muscle tone can be reduced significantly with training. Relaxation means no muscular activity at all or getting as near to zero activity as possible.

You may be wondering why any athlete would want to be completely relaxed. What has relaxation got to do with competitive sport? Athletes need a certain amount of arousal. In some sports, they need maximal arousal to accomplish their task. Most athletes believe if they train hard and have good workouts, they will sleep well and be able to relax without learning specific relaxation skills. This is not necessarily so. In fact, sleeping is not necessarily relaxing. If your bed looks as though you have been sleeping with two tigers all night with pillows and bed covers all askew, you have not had a restful night of sleep. The condition of your bed in the morning is a good indicator of how much tension you are experiencing during sleep.

Relaxation is a skill that must be learned. In the process you develop a much greater sensitivity to your bodily feelings and responses. Once you learn to attend to somatic responses and learn to associate these responses with certain types of behavior you can learn to deal with your environment actively and effectively. You will have control and can regulate your responses to whatever situation you encounter. Relaxation is not the panacea for all situations. Obviously, there are situations where arousal,

Relaxation means letting go and doing absolutely nothing with your muscles.

tension and mental concern are appropriate and realistic responses. However, when you learn that too much of such a response can be counter productive to your behavior, you need to learn how to regulate your response so you have just enough to maximize the performance.

Once you have learned the skill, you can use relaxation techniques to lower general muscular activity under any condition where you are aware of producing too much. You will be able to remove localized tension such as that occurring with tension headaches or lower back pain. Relaxation will facilitate recovery when you have only a short time to rest. You can use this immediately following a workout, between events in your sport, during breaks, or anywhere and at any time you wish to "catch your breath" and recharge your batteries a bit. Relaxation also promotes sleep. If you are the type of person who can set the stage for going to sleep but lie there tossing, turning and looking at the clock hour after hour, relaxation will help you get right to sleep! Probably the most important contribution that relaxation can make to you as an athlete is to teach you how to regulate your arousal so that you do not over-charge the system.

To learn to relax you must practice on a regular basis just as you would any sport skill. If you do not continue to use it, you tend to lose the skill. There are several different approaches and techniques that have been developed to teach relaxation. Some of these approaches work better for one than another. All of them will be discussed in this section. The important thing is to find one that works for you and use it!

In general, the techniques of relaxation can be divided into two categories: First, the techniques that focus on the somatic aspects or those that are considered "muscle to mind." Jacobson's scientific neuromuscular relaxation or progressive relaxation would fall under this category. The object is to train the muscles to become sensitive to any level of tension. You learn this by generating as much tension as possible, letting it go, and studying the difference in the muscle.

The second category of techniques includes all those that approach relaxation from the cognitive or mental perspective. These work from "mind to muscle." Herbert Benson's relaxation response, transcendental meditation, autogenic training, and imagery all approach relaxation from the cognitive focus.

Either approach is effective; you need to experiment to discover which works best for you. Athletes, because they are more somatically aware, tend to learn Jacobson's progressive relaxation much more readily than those who are not tuned into their bodies. Athletes are used to working with their muscles and already know what maximal tension feels like for the most part. As a result, this technique will be discussed first.

Progressive Relaxation: Muscle to Mind

Scientific neuromuscular relaxation or progressive relaxation is a technique developed by Dr. Edmund Jacobson. It is called progressive because you progress from one muscle group to another as you learn the skill. The skill is learned by inducing as much tension as possible into one muscle group, learning to identify what tension feels like, then "letting it go" so all the tension is released. Your attention is focused on the muscle and on becoming sensitive enough to tension so you can identify any level of tension in any muscle. Once you have learned this skill, you do not continue to "manufacture" tension before you relax. That technique is only for learning the skill. After you become sensitive to any and every degree of tension, you will automatically identify tension and let it go without being conscious of doing so. That is the goal of becoming trained in progressive relaxation.

Let us try a little experiment. Hyperextend you hand back as though you are trying to place the back of your hand on your forearm. You may sense a feeling of some sort in the wrist joint which is probably strain. You will feel something else in the muscle which is tension. Let the tension go allowing the hand to drop completely relaxed. Now try it again, contract the muscles of the forearm hard so the hand is pulled back as far as possible. Let it go again and try to distinguish the difference you feel in the muscle from being tense to being relaxed. Repeat it again but put only half as much tension in the muscle. See if you can determine what half as much is, identify it, then let it go. This time put one-fourth as much tension in the muscles, hold, then let go. Now put just enough tension in the muscle to feel it. It may take maximal tension for you, less than one-fourth of maximal, or just thinking about tension there. Focus on identifying what it feels like, then let it go. Now, just imagine that you are putting tension in the muscles and see if you can feel it, then let it go.

Basically, that is the principle of neuromuscular relaxation. You progress through one muscle group after another: arms, hands, legs, shoulders, thighs, back, facial, and so on. With each group you focus on training the muscle to become sensitive to varying degrees of tension, identifying that tension, and then letting it go and trying to maintain that feeling without allowing tension to come back into the muscle. You will become sensitive to the tension in somewhat the same way that a blind person develops a sensitivity to raised dots in the Braille alphabet through the fingertips. You will learn to detect even the slightest tension and begin to adjust and let go automatically without any conscious awareness. During the learning process you will continue to create tension and let it go so that you can learn to recognize and distinguish the difference between the two. As indicated, once you learn to identify it, you can let it go from that point; you do not have to manufacture more to let go!

Now try another experiment. Assume a relaxed sitting posture, legs uncrossed, feet flat on the floor, arms and hands placed in the lap. Let your head fall forward as though you have fallen asleep. Let it hang naturally, do not try to hold it in a certain position. Your body should be supported by the chair in such a way that you would not fall out of the chair if you were shot. Now make the biggest grimace you can with your face, tightening all the muscles, closing the eyes tightly. Hold it momentarily and let it go. Repeat, this time paying close attention to what happens to the eyes. Just for a split second they should remain motionless and relaxed. Try it again and see if you can identify this feeling. Now in the same relaxed position, mentally think through something you memorized a long time ago. Can you feel any tension in your eyes? If you are sensitive enough to tension you will be able to detect some accompanying the movement of the eyes. If this happened, you have just discovered that you cannot think without tension. You literally think with your muscles. This fact allows researchers to know when someone is dreaming; they use rapid eye movements (REM) as the indicator. You do not dream or process anything cognitively without some muscular tension. Tension is necessary for expressing thoughts and words. When you learn to relax the facial muscles, eye muscles, the tongue, vocal cords and throat muscles you can stop thought! Just think, if you learn to do that, never again will your thoughts keep you awake! All you have to do is relax all those muscle groups and your thoughts stop!

Another advantage of learning to relax with this technique is the ability to stop what we call "double-thinking." Most of us have been in situations where our eyes have followed the words across page after page. Yet, when we finish, we do not know what we have read because we have been thinking about something else all the time we were reading. By learning to relax all the muscles except those needed for the task at hand, you can stop the double-thinking. You can get rid of all the sensory input and nerve activity that is "jamming the programmer." Not only can you use relaxation to fall asleep, you can also use it to help in concentration. You will find that you can study much more effectively and will need less time to learn the same amount of material.

In addition to progressive relaxation, which means relaxing all muscle groups as completely as you can, there is differential relaxation. Differential relaxation means that you learn to relax all the muscles except those that are needed for the task at hand. This is very important in sport skills where appropriate form means using the least amount of energy to accomplish the skill. A good test of whether you can do this or not is when you are doing weight training. If you can relax all the muscles except the group you are working, you have accomplished differential relaxation. Few can do this; most of the athletes in the weight room are throwing their bodies all over the place while they are working one muscle group!

With proper training in progressive relaxation you can accomplish differential relaxation as you become sensitive to tension in all muscle groups. When you use conscious control (which is what progressive relaxation is) you relax deeply but you do not go to sleep. You may discover that you will not have thought of anything because the muscles necessary for thought will have been too relaxed to allow cognitive or mental processing. With proper training you will be able to snatch a little "brain rest" most any place during a busy day. After a few seconds of complete relaxation you can snap back to increased alertness with greater energy. This is a much better way to rest than taking a nap. After a nap many people need an hour or so to wake up and get back to a functional level. Not so with progressive relaxation!

When you are learning and practicing relaxation techniques you may become aware of little twitches or spasms in your muscles. These are produced when the shortened fibers that are tense begin to let go. At times you may have a whole muscle group let go at once and your arm or leg may move voluntarily as the muscle fibers let go. If you are lying down, you may feel your buttock muscles let go which will produce a feeling of sinking into the mat or floor. In each case, the muscle fibers have relaxed sufficiently to let go. As you become trained in relaxation, you will discover that you do not build up as much residual tension. As a result, you are more relaxed throughout the day and do not have as much muscular tension to eliminate when you do relax. This will reduce the number of twitches and spasms you experience.

With practice you can acquire the fine art of conserving energies scientifically by applying basic physiological principles. You will have learned a new type of self-control that will become a habitual response to unnecessary tension.

How to Do Progressive Relaxation
There are many modifications of progressive relaxation exercises, however each requires a certain type of environment and certain conditions to maximize the training. Find a relatively quiet, distraction-free area that has a comfortable temperature. It is virtually impossible to relax in a cold room! You may have the lights dimmed if you wish; however, that is not necessary. Remove or loosen any tight clothing; you can also remove your shoes if you desire. If you wear hard contact lenses, you may wish to remove them as you can relax more easily with your eyes closed. If you have an injured muscle, you may want to avoid generating as much tension as you can in that muscle group. Make sure you position yourself so the injured portion of your body is supported and comfortable.

Each approach to progressive relaxation requires that you get into a comfortable position, preferably lying on your back on a mat on the floor. Ideally, you want the floor to support your body in such a way that no muscle group has to work to support any segment. Relax your hips, thighs, and legs in such a manner that your feet flop out towards you little-toe side. Your arms should be alongside your body, slightly flexed at the elbows. Your hands will also be slightly flexed in a relaxed position. You may find that a pillow or some support placed under your knees will be more confortable. A support for the neck may increase the comfort as well.

It is easier to learn to relax after you have had a good physical workout. Exercise, in itself, tends to reduce anxiety and tension. As a result, learning to relax after exercise is a good way to begin. Once you have learned the skill, you can relax anywhere at anytime! In fact, once you are trained, you may find that relaxing just before a practice helps you to concentrate better. In addition to getting a rest, you can eliminate all the thoughts that tend to disrupt concentration during practice. This does not mean that they will go away; it just means that you can get away from them for awhile!

The initial training program designed by Jacobson required much more time in training each respective muscle group than most of the modifications. Regardless of the modification, the training progresses from one muscle group to another beginning with the muscles of the dominant hand and forearm. As in any relaxation technique, you should get into a comfortable position in a quiet and comfortable environment where you will not be disturbed. Let your eyes close gradually as you let go and allow your body to be totally supported by the mat (or chair if you are sitting). Use the first lessons with more detailed instructions as the model for the remaining lessons. You should spend approximately thirty minutes with each lesson. You will soon learn to adjust the time of the tension and the pause for relaxation before the next instruction. The larger muscle groups are tensed for longer periods of time than the smaller muscles of the eyes, jaws and feet.

Hands and Arms (Lesson 1)
- Bend the hand of the dominant arm back, fingers straight, as though you are trying to place the back of your hand on your forearm.
- Hold that position for approximately 10 seconds, relax and let go.
- Identify where the tension is felt. Repeat.
- Now bend the hand in such a way that you are trying to touch your fingers to the underside of your forearm. Hold, feel the tension, relax and let go. Repeat.
- Repeat the whole sequence with the other arm.
- Repeat the sequence with both arms with half as much tension, relaxing slowly.
- Repeat with just enough tension to identify it, hold, relax and let go.
- From the forearm muscles, move to the dominant upper arm repeating the sequence, flexing the elbow to put tension in the biceps. Begin with maximal tension, relax, repeat.
- Repeat again with half as much tension, relax and repeat.
- Repeat with just enough tension to identify, relax, and repeat.
- Repeat sequence with non-dominant arm.
- Repeat sequence with arms.
- Focusing on the extensor muscles of the arm, press down against the floor with both wrists, hold, and relax. Repeat the

sequence with half as much tension and just enough tension to identify.

- Using both arms, slowly increase the tension from fingertips to shoulders without moving. Tighten a little bit more, still more, and continue to gradually increase tension until it is as tense and rigid as you can make it with fists clenched tightly. Hold, and slowly let the tension go a little bit at a time, a little bit more, continuing until the arms are completely free of tension. Continue to relax more and more.
- Repeat tension and relaxation with only half as much tension and then with just enough to identify the tension.

Exercise, in itself, tends to reduce anxiety and tension.

LESSON	MUSCLE GROUP	INSTRUCTIONS
2 (30 Minutes)	Feet and Legs	Bend (flex) right foot trying to put big toe against shin bone. Hold, quickly let go and relax. Repeat. Repeat sequence with half as much tension, hold, relax. Repeat with just enough tension to identify, hold, relax. Repeat entire sequence with left foot. Pointing the toes, repeat the entire sequence with right, left, then both feet. Repeat the sequence lifting the legs slightly above the floor. Repeat sequence pressing the feet and legs against the mat as hard as you can.
3 (30 Minutes)	Abdominal, Back and Buttocks	Review beginning with making a fist, hold, relax. Put as much tension as possible in both hands and arms, hold relax. Put as much tension as possible in legs and feet, hold, relax. Pull in abdominal muscles slowly, hold, quickly relax. Repeat. Pull in with half the effort, hold, relax slowly. Repeat with one-fourth effort. Tighten your buttocks hard, hold, relax quickly. Repeat with half and then one-fourth effort, relax. Tighten just enough to feel, relax. Tense the abdominal muscles just enough to feel tension, hold, relax quickly. Arch back slowly, hold, quickly relax. Repeat. Arch with half the effort, hold, relax slowly. Repeat with one-fourth effort. Now simply imagine you are arching your back slowly as high as you can. Hold, then quickly relax and let go of all tensions. Continuing to relax, take a deep breath, hold, identify tension, breathe out naturally. Take a deep breath, hold, let go quickly and note air leaves in a puff. Continue breathing normally while relaxing more and more with each exhalation.

LESSON	MUSCLE GROUP	INSTRUCTIONS
4 (30 Minutes)	Shoulders and Neck	Push shoulder and head against mat, hold, relax quickly. Repeat using half, then one-fourth the amount of effort. Try to pull shoulders together in front of your chest, hold, relax quickly. Repeat with half the effort, hold, relax slowly. Repeat with just enough effort to feel it, hold, relax quickly. Shrug your shoulders up to your ears, hold, relax quickly. Repeat with half the effort and then one-fourth the effort. Shrug your shoulders with just enough tension to feel, hold, relax quickly. Press your head against the mat hard, hold, relax quickly. Repeat with half, one-fourth, and then just enough tension to identify. Try to put your right ear on your right shoulder, hold, relax. Repeat with half, one-fourth, and then just enough tension to feel, relax. Repeat entire sequence to the left side.
5 (30 Minutes)	Facial and Eye	Raise eyebrows slowly as far as you can, hold, relax quickly. Repeat and relax slowly. Repeat again with just enough tension to identify. Knit your brow drawing the brows together, hold, relax quickly. Repeat with just enough tension to feel, hold, relax slowly. Frown with just enough tension to identify, hold, relax quickly. Close eyelids tightly but slowly, hold, relax quickly. Repeat, hold, relax slowly. Imagine you are closing your eyes tightly, hold, relax. Close just tight enough to feel tension, hold, relax slowly. Make the biggest grimace you can, tensing all the muscles of the face and eyes, hold, and relax quickly. Repeat with just enough tension to identify. Keeping your eyes closed, look to the right as far as you can, hold briefly, relax, and let your eyes center normally. Repeat looking to the left, looking up and looking down. Imagine watching a tennis match seated at the side of the court where the net post is located. Let your eyes follow the ball back and forth, note the tension, relax and let the eyes center normally. Imagine looking for someone in a dark theatre, identify the tension, relax.

LESSON	MUSCLE GROUP	INSTRUCTIONS
6 (30 Minutes)	Jaws and Throat	Clench teeth closing jaws firmly, hold, relax quickly. Repeat relaxing slowly. Clench just enough to feel the tension, hold, relax quickly. Repeat. Pucker lips as if to whistle, hold, quickly relax. Repeat relaxing slowly. Pucker just enough to feel tension, hold, relax quickly. Smile broadly, quickly relax. Smile slowly and slowly relax. Repeat smile with just enough tension to feel, relax quickly. Push tongue against your front teeth, hold, quickly relax. Repeat with half and one-fourth effort, hold, relax slowly. Repeat with just enough tension to identify, hold, relax quickly. Pull tongue back into throat, hold, relax quickly. Repeat with half and one-fourth the effort, hold, relax quickly. Let the jaw muscles go slack so that the teeth separate, maintain that let go feeling without letting tension come back.

Instructions for Progressive Relaxation

- For best results, have someone read the instructions to you. If this is not possible, make a tape for yourself.
- When reading the instructions, maintain a normal voice pattern, pacing the instructions by doing the exercises as you read. In so doing, you will establish a suitable pace. Make sure you hold the tension long enough to feel and identify it, then relax. Pause between instructions so that relaxation can continue for brief periods without being interrupted by the next instruction. Tense large muscle groups longer than small muscle groups.
- Remember, the production of tension is for learning the relaxation technique. Once you have learned to identify any level of tension in the muscle, you can relax from that point without producing additional tension.
- Faithful practice beyond the instruction is essential to learning the skill. Practice whenever you can, especially when you are trying to rest and when going to sleep. Practice differential relaxation at all times.
- If you feel restless and uncomfortable, that is an indication of excessive body tension. Try to find a comfortable position without any joints being flexed or ankles crossed and let the mat support your body completely.
- If you feel that you cannot tolerate thirty minutes of doing "nothing", you need to focus on your breathing and try to let go of tension in muscle groups. Impatience, irritability, restlessness, and squirming are all signs of excessive tension.
- When you are relaxed your breathing becomes slow and regular, pulse rate decreases, and you may not hear the instructions after a while. Most instructors will usually ask you to signal in some manner such as raising a forefinger when you have relaxed a particular muscular group. Do not worry about missing some of the instructions. That is a normal response as you begin to enjoy the feeling that deep relaxation produces. You just want to enjoy this state without having it disrupted. You have no desire to leave this blissful state!
- You will be without a facial expression as the muscles become completely relaxed; the eyes may open partly when the face becomes absolutely blank, evidencing no thought patterns.
- You will lose track of time and not know whether ten minutes or half an hour has passed. You will also move into a relaxed

state where you are not aware of any thought processing. That is the desired state of relaxation that you are trying to reach.

- Repetition is the key to learning, continue to practice the same procedure for muscle groups until you can relax very quickly without producing additional tension.
- Some individuals become anxious about relaxing because they think they are losing control. Do not worry about this. When you learn to relax you acquire control rather than losing it! You are out of control when you cannot eliminate tension when you wish to.
- Do not try to hold any body part still. That takes effort and tension! Let the mat or chair do the supporting and holding.
- Be patient when you have a practice session where you feel that you are not accomplishing anything. Think about how many times you have practiced a sports skill before it just happens naturally. Relaxation is learned the same way.
- End each relaxation session by taking five deep breaths at your own rate of speed. With each breath feel the energy flowing into your muscles and activating your system so that you feel alert and rested after the session. Some find that a good stretch (much like that of cats) activates the system and prepares you for activity after relaxation. Use whatever works best for you.
- In short, relaxation is not magic. It is a skill that must be learned and practiced to be effective. Once learned so that your body is sensitive to varying levels of tension, you begin to automatically adjust levels downward when too much tension occurs. Theoretically, you should never have a "nervous breakdown" once you are trained in relaxation, as you would never reach that point of overload.

Additional Relaxation Techniques: Mind to Muscle

The majority of other relaxation techniques focus on the mental control or the efferent nerve control. That is, the focus is on controlling the stimulation from the central nervous system to the muscle. This, in turn, leads to relaxation of the muscles. Progressive relaxation, on the other hand, focuses on the afferent portion of the nerves, reducing the stimulation to the brain which reduces the mental stimulation, producing relaxation. The end result is the same since approximately one half of the nerves are afferent or *to* the central nervous system and the other half efferent or *from* the central nervous system. Reducing the sensation in either half will interrupt the circuit of stimulation necessary to produce tension in the muscles.

The major techniques in this category include meditation, Benson's relaxation response, autogenic training, and the use of imagery or visualization. Each of these will be discussed in some detail.

Meditation

Meditation is a cognitive or mental technique for relaxation which utilizes the mind to muscle approach. Basically, it involves using a mantra which is a non-stimulating, meaningless sound of one or two syllables. The purpose of the mantra is to provide a focus for your attention. You are to focus your attention in a very passive manner. As has been discussed earlier, you think with your muscles and when you are thinking about something interesting and stimulating (or bothersome), you have difficulty relaxing. A mantra provides a non-stimulating focus so that your attention does not go from one thing to another. If your mind tends to wander, passively return to focusing on the mantra.

During the time that you focus your attention on the mantra you are to sit quietly and comfortably with your eyes closed. It is recommended that you spend at least twenty minutes twice a day meditating. Once you have learned the skill, you can meditate anywhere. Keep in mind that you are not to force the attentional focus on the mantra, just let it happen! In a passive sense, you are to experience the mantra, just let it consume you.

When your attention is completely focused on the mantra you eliminate many, if not most, of the efferent signals from the brain to muscles, organs, etc. As a result, your somatic responses tend to become more quiet. It is the uncontrolled cognitive processing that keeps your body aroused. Further, with a mantra, you reduce the amount of stimulation being sent to the central nervous system and the brain. This produces a relaxing effect as well. When you focus on a meaningless sound, a mantra, you do not generate arousing thoughts that activate your system. If your mind does wander, and it will as you practice, don't worry about it. When your attention wanders, just remind yourself to refocus on the mantra.

Meditation is one way to "rest the central nervous system" and can be used anytime when you can take fifteen or twenty minutes to disregard whatever is going on around you. Practicing meditation is a good way to increase your concentration. Once skills are well learned in sport, you do not have to think about them, you just let them happen. Meditation is good practice for "letting things happen." You learn to be "aware but not aware of your awareness." In short, you learn to be engulfed by the action of the game in such a way that you do not need to concentrate on what you are doing because it happens automatically.

Relaxation Responses

Benson, a physician at Harvard Medical School, literally took the "hokus pokus" jargon out of meditation and explained it in a simple, everyday manner. The principles are the same as those in meditation. Regardless of whether one is meditating (as discussed previously) or practicing the relaxation response, there are four basic elements. First, you need a quiet environment where external stimulation and distraction are reduced. The temperature should be comfortable as well as the atmosphere.

The second element is to have something to dwell upon or to focus your attention on during the relaxation period. Benson suggests that you can use a word such as "one" and continue to repeat that over and over. If your mind wanders, let it pass on through and come back to thinking about "one." However, using the word "one" with athletes does not provide a non-stimulating cue! Some begin to immediately think of "being number one," of being first! Make sure you select a word that will not stimulate your thoughts to take off to other associations of the word. You might select a symbol to focus upon. A particular feeling can also be used for focus. The point is to have something upon which to direct your thoughts which does not produce a whole series of stimulating associations in your mind. Some individuals find that focusing on their breathing works, thinking "relax" as they breathe in and "let go" as they breathe out again. Regardless of the object you select for focus, if your mind wanders, let those thoughts pass on through. Do not try to hang on to them, just let your thoughts passively return to your focus object.

The third basic element concerns a passive attitude. Benson feels this is the most important element. You have to learn to let it happen, to let those thoughts and images that come into your mind pass on through in a very passive manner, making no attempt to attend to them. Just return passively to your object of attention. Do not worry about how many times your mind wanders. Each time passively let it return to the object you have selected for focus.

A comfortable position is the fourth element of the relaxation response. You should try to find a comfortable position to assume, however, you do not want to become so comfortable that you fall asleep.

The relaxation response can be used in the same manner as meditation by the athlete. Again, if it works, use it!

Autogenic Training

Autogenic suggests self-induced responses and utilizes a combination of "mind to muscle" and "muscle to mind" approaches in developing a deep state of relaxation. The technique was developed in Germany in the early 1930's and has been used extensively with the European athletes. The training consists of a series of exercises designed to produce two physical sensations, that of warmth and heaviness. Basically, it is a technique of auto-hypnosis or self-hypnosis. Your attention is focused on the sensations you are trying to produce. As in meditation, you just let them happen in a passive manner. There are six stages in training, each stage should be learned before progressing to the next stage. Some suggest that two weeks should be spent in training at each stage, however, you can modify that to suit your own rate of learning. It usually takes several months of regular practice of ten to forty minutes, one to six times per day to become proficient enough to experience heaviness and warmth in your limbs and to produce a sensation of a relaxed, calm heartbeat and respiratory rate accompanied by warmth in the abdomen and coolness in your forehead. Once you have learned that and attain a relaxed state, you can use imagery to increase the depth of relaxation.

Three basic body positions are recommended for autogenic training. As in any type of relaxation, all distractions and discomforts should be eliminated in the environment and there should be no restrictions with regard to clothing, jewelry, contact lenses or shoes. Of the three body positions, the easiest position is the lying down one, allowing the surface on which one is lying to support the body completely. Legs should be relaxed with feet inclined outward, arms extended along the body, elbows slightly flexed and hands relaxed. If need be, support the back of the neck, small of the back, and/or back of knees to ensure maximal comfort.

The other two positions involve sitting. The first one in a straight back chair that is high enough to support the neck and back of the head. The depth should be such that the buttocks are supported by the back of the chair and the thighs are supported by the seat. Arms may be supported by the arms of the chair or hang loosely alongside the body. The feet should be supported by the floor.

The second sitting position is on a stool in a balanced and supported position. Sit forward, feet firmly planted, knees shoulder's width apart with lower arms resting on thighs with fingers and hands dangling in a relaxed position. The head and shoulders drop forward in a position that does not place any strain on the back or stomach areas.

From any one of these positions, the same six stages are followed for the exercises. The first stage involves focusing your attention in a passive manner on your dominant arm while silently saying, "My right (left) arm is heavy" three to five times during one minute. Flex your arms and move your body about, then repeat the sequence with the non-dominant arm, then with the dominant leg, followed by the non-dominant leg. A sense of heaviness should take over your body. If your mind wanders, passively redirect your attention back to the task at hand. You may be able to produce a sense of heaviness immediately or you may take one or two weeks of three or more times of practice daily to accomplish it.

Once you have mastered the heaviness exercise you can move to the warmth stage. The warmth exercise follows the exact same procedures as the heaviness exercises, starting with the dominant arm. Many individuals require more training to establish a sensation of warmth in all of their extremities, some take as long as four weeks.

Regulation of the heartbeat is the third stage after you have mastered the heaviness and warmth exercise. Take a minute or two for the instructions of saying, "My heartbeat is calm and regular" with a break from the focus of concentration between four repeats of the exercise. Once this exercise has been mastered, you move to the fourth stage of regulating your breathing rate. You may have already noticed that your breathing has become slower and more regular with the previous exercises. However, now focus your attention on your respiration rate in a passive manner using the instruction, "It breathes me." Again, repeat four times for a period of approximately two minutes each with a break between.

The fifth stage of exercise is designed to induce a sensation of warmth to the abdominal region which produces a calming effect on the central nervous system and enhances overall muscular relaxation. You may place your hand upon the upper abdominal region while silently saying, "My solar plexis is warm." Repeat this four times with the appropriate breaks between exercises. The final stage involves concentrating on the forehead and saying, "My forehead is cool." The same procedure of four repeats with breaks between is followed.

In summary, the stages for autogenic training are as follows:

Stage 1:   Heaviness
             My right arm is heavy.
             My left arm is heavy.
             Both arms are heavy.
             My right leg is heavy.
             My left leg is heavy.
             Both legs are heavy.
             My arms and legs are very heavy.

Stage 2:   Warmth
             The instructions follow as in Heaviness.

Stage 3:   Heart rate regulation
             My heartbeat is regular and calm.

Stage 4:   Breathing Rate
             My breathing rate is slow, calm, and relaxed, "It breathes me."

Stage 5:   Warmth in the solar plexis
             My solar plexis is warm (hand placed on upper abdominal area).

Stage 6:   Forehead
             My forehead is cool.

It may take you anywhere from two months to a year to master these skills. As you become more proficient, you can combine the six stages, completing the entire series in a matter of minutes. Regular daily practice for several minutes three or four times a day is recommended for training.

After you have mastered the six stages and can induce the desired state in a few minutes and sustain it for thirty minutes to an hour, you are ready to move to the next stage of training which is called "autogenic meditation." Basically, this involves imagery of visualization. The first exercise is a voluntary rotation of the eyes in an upward and inward position which increases the percent of brain alpha waves. The second stage focuses on the ability to visualize color. You should try to statically hold a color that occupies your entire visual field in your mind's eye. From a static exercise, you can move to visualizing colors in movement or formations.

Once you have mastered those skills, the third exercise involves visualizing and holding an image of a particular object in a static position. Once that has been mastered you can move to the fourth exercise which consists of visualizing some abstract concept such as happiness, or confidence, or the like.

Following several weeks of training at each of these stages, you can move to the fifth stage of exercises where you will practice experiencing a chosen state of feeling. This can be a mind-body feeling that you experience in sport such as "flow" or winning, or a peak experience when everything goes just right! Your concentration should be passive, just let it happen, with the focus on the general, overall feeling.

The sixth and final stage of training in autogenic meditation includes visualizing other people. This exercise can be readily applied to sport situations where you can visualize your opponent(s) and/or teammates. However, the recommended approach is to visualize relatively neutral individuals before moving on to significant other or others with whom there might be conflict. See the chapter on "instant replays" elsewhere in this book for further suggestions and directions.

As indicated earlier, autogenic training takes a relatively long time to master. As a result, it is less popular in the United States because athletes are not training under the same coach for such long periods of time. It is used extensively in many of the East European countries where athletes are housed in sports training centers for several years working with a relatively stable staff of coaches and sports medicine personnel. Despite the time required to become proficient in all the skills, you may find it a satisfactory means of training for relaxation and imagery. If you find that you respond to auto-suggestions, this technique will be appealing to you.

Focus on Breathing
Many of the relaxation techniques incorporate a focus on breath-

ing. This provides a cue that is always with you; if not, it doesn't matter whether you relax or not! Your attentional focus should be on the inhalation and exhalation trying to increase the sensation of relaxation with each inhalation and letting go of more and more tension throughout the body with each exhalation. If your mind wanders between breaths (and it will), passively let those thoughts pass on through without attending to them and return your focus to your breathing. This approach to relaxation has been used by many athletes with a great deal of success.

Visualization
Another successful technique for those who can visualize easily has been imagining that you are in a place conducive to relaxation. You can visualize lying on a beach in the warm sun, or a beautiful mountain scene, or whatever provides you with a sense of relaxation. The rule of thumb with any approach to relaxation is, 'If it works, use it!" See the chapter on "Instant Replay."

Music
The idea that music can influence your mind and body has been around for centuries; babies have been lullabied to sleep, recruits chant cadence with physical training runs, music has accompanied harvesting to relieve the fatigue of labor and religion has used music throughout the rituals to ease the burdens of life. The rhythms of music have been used to carry both people and animals into altered states of consciousness.

Specific forms of music with specific rhythms can induce a relaxed state of mind. Classical music has been used, particularly that of the Baroque period, to slow down and synchronize the breathing and heart rate patterns. This, in turn, lowers the blood pressure and increases the percent of alpha waves.

Johann Sebastian Bach composed a series of pieces for the Russian envoy Count Kayserling to reduce his insomnia. The Count became rested and less tense and was able to fall asleep quickly when this music was played for him. He was so pleased with the results that he rewarded Bach with a large amount of gold. Music written by other composers of the sixteenth to eighteenth centuries produced similar effects. In addition to Bach, Telemann, Handel, Vivaldi and Corelli composed Baroque music. The concertos of this period are characterized by different segments played at different speeds. The slow movements produce a rhythm of sixty beats per minute, often with a slow bass which tends to synchronize the heart and breath rates. Listening to this music, letting it consume you in a passive manner, relaxes you in a holistic way. You do not have to be conscious of instructing the muscles to relax nor do you have to repeat a mantra or concentrate on cognitive control. There is little variation in the 4/4 time and the sixty beats per minute sections of Baroque concertos that produce this effect. You can prepare your own tape of these segments to form a relaxation tape.

Obviously, different beats in music produce difference responses and commercial advertising and theater capitalize on this fact to influence behavior. Music can arouse, irritate, frustrate, or produce a variety of responses. However, only the particularly slow segments of the Baroque period appear to produce the total bodily response to relaxation accompanied by alertness and increased awareness for maximizing learning while relaxing. The book *Superlearning* explains in detail the procedures for using Baroque music to relax and increase learning at the same time.

Other types of music are written specifically for relaxation and produce that effect as well, without the added component of increased alertness and learning ability. Music has been written to generate all types of mood states. If you can find music that relaxes you, use it for that purpose. The object is to find a strategy or technique that you can utilize in all situations when you desire to relax. With the availability of sound systems in headsets, you can have music available anywhere without disturbing those around you.

When to Use Relaxation

As mentioned earlier, you can use relaxation to lower general muscular activity, remove localized tension, facilitate rest, promote sleep, and to regulate arousal to produce optimal levels for maximizing performance.

You can learn best after a physical workout as exercise tends to be one of nature's best tranquilizers. In sport, the training sessions should be at the end of the physical practice. Once the skills have been learned, the practice can be started with a relaxation session to ease the accumulation of stresses and anxieties and "clear the flak" out of the system. Concentration will be improved which will increase the quality of the practice. You will discover you can accomplish much more in less time, thus reducing the overall practice time. Using relaxation in combination with concentration, imagery and self-talk prior to practice will increase the ability to concentrate to a greater extent.

You must determine what your optimal level of arousal is for maximizing your performance before you can utilize relaxation techniques properly prior to practices and competitions that you view important. One way to establish this marker is to keep a daily record of how you feel and perform to determine what pattern of feelings produces the performance that is consistently at a high level. Once you have determined this, you can regulate your arousal using relaxation to control it.

Sometimes during practice, instead of trying harder, you need to relax and just let it happen. Putting too much effort into skill execution is almost always counter productive. Frequently, when you are having trouble with a skill, taking a few minutes out to relax in combination with imagery will be more productive than repeating the skill over and over when you are tense, fatigued or not concentrating.

During the competition you can utilize differential relaxation techniques to improve your form by using only those muscles necessary to do the skill and using only the necessary amount of tension for a seemingly effortless movement. This will reduce and possibly eliminate mental errors, turnovers, overhitting, using too much force, losing your "touch" or "choking." Relaxation does not reduce "aggressiveness." In fact, it improves your alertness and awareness in such a way that your performance will be maximized and you can play your best without "foaming at the mouth" and having glazed-over eyes.

Relaxation techniques should be used when traveling to reduce fatigue so you can arrive at the competition site rested. Depending on how long you must travel and the mode and conditions of travel, the ability to relax may well make the difference between a successful and unsuccessful competition. Some athletes are not good flyers and every flight for them is a "white knuckle" one. In this day of air travel and national and international competition, you must learn to relax during the flights.

Another tremendous advantage of learning to relax is the promotion of sleep. Insomnia among athletes is extensive; many say that they cannot sleep away from home or even at home the night before a competition. Relaxation techniques will eliminate tensions and the thoughts that keep you awake. The ability to relax will also aid in sleeping when you have pain.

In short, learning to hang loose in all situations is taking one giant step toward playing at consistently high levels at or near your potential performance. The time spent during practice in learning how to relax will pay off many times over throughout your years of participation. If time is not spent in practice, then make the time on your own to learn how to relax. There are many tapes available with instructions for relaxation. Select one that you find useful for you or make your own using the instructions included here or in many of the references listed in the back of this book. Having someone else provide the instructions is the most effective means of learning. When that is not available, tapes provide the next best learning conditions. It is difficult to read the instructions and then try to relax without the aid of external instructions because you have to stay cognitively aware to "program" your own directions for muscle groups. The most effective way is to "just let it happen" by passively listening to someone else provide the instructions for you to follow.

4

CONCENTRATION: DIRECTING YOUR ATTENTIONAL FOCUS

One of the biggest problems in sport, whether it be competitive or recreational, is a lack of concentration. A wandering mind can create mental lapses and cause mental errors during any performance. Many times you hear an athlete say, "I lost my concentration, I just couldn't get it back together." Or, a coach will say, "They lost their concentration and lost the momentum." Coaches are notorious for attributing lack of an athlete's or team's success to loss of concentration. Everyone knows what concentration is. The concept is understood by all, yet its meaning is quite subtle. One cannot concentrate on concentration; that defeats the entire process. A coach who demands more concentration from you without teaching the skill is trying to demand something that the mind has not been trained to do. A coach would not demand performance of a complex physical skill that had never been taught!

Concentration or paying attention to what you are doing and what is going on is a skill that can be learned and it must be practiced regularly to be maintained at a high level of efficiency. Sport, by its very nature, enhances concentration but specific practice improves it beyond that point. Among athletes, or any other group, great individual differences exist in ability to focus and attend to something over a length of time. Coaches and athletes alike need to plan their practices and work on the more difficult and complex new material and information early in their practice period.

Concentration or selective attention involves being able to attend to what is going on, the degree to which you can attend, and how long you can continue to attend to what is going on around you. Selective attention is being able to choose to attend to specific things going on and to ignore others, or the ability to put the mind on one thing at a time or on all the things that relate to what is going on at that time. The more you have the ability to attend to what you want to, the better the response and the performance.

If you are not focused one hundred percent on what you are doing, then performance cannot be maximized. When you are concentrating and giving your undivided attention to the task at hand you are aware of nothing else. Some athletes explain this state by saying things such as, "I felt spacey, as though I was not even there." Others describe it as a situation where things slow down and one has all the time in the world to execute and perform. They feel and see exactly what is happening and they know what is going to happen next. Others say, "I wasn't even aware of anything, it was as though I was not even thinking about what was going on, it just happened. I saw and felt everything, things just happened without my having to think about them." Some athletes feel capable of doing anything they wish; everything goes just right without any special effort.

Attention

Attention, rather than concentration, is the term used in psychology to describe the process which you use to perceive the outside world. Attention has several dimensions. One aspect is how diffused or how concentrated your attention is. Your attention can be spread over many stimuli or it can be concentrated on one particular point. The nature of the sport or the specific demands of a particular position will alter the dimension of your concentration. As an example, a basketball player taking a free throw should have attention focused on the rim of the goal and on what it takes to put the ball through that hoop. A quarterback, on the other hand, needs to have his attention spread over many different stimuli. He needs to be able to scan an array of relevant cues. He needs to be able to read his opponent's defenses, to call an audible if need be, to pick out his primary receiver, then move to his secondary receiver if necessary. He needs to concentrate on all of these relevant cues in a matter of seconds in order to perform his task.

Some athletes appear to have "eyes in the back of their heads" because they can focus their attention and process relevant cues without distractions and interference. Others have difficulty in paying attention to where their opponents are and where their teammates are. Athletes can be observed passing to their opponents or failing to see their own teammates who are wide open and trying to attract their attention for a pass. Athletes who are not attending properly fail to see pass or play options because they are not picking up relevant cues.

Another aspect of concentration or the attentional process concerns the degree of alertness. An athlete may be very alert and respond quickly and easily to the situation. In the same situation, another athlete may be inattentive to available stimuli and slow to respond even when the coach and the spectators are providing advice and direction. A good athlete has to learn to be fully aware of what is going on and to pay attention to and respond to relevant cues on time without being distracted.

The cues selected for attention provide yet another aspect of the attentional process. As an athlete, you have to isolate certain cues for more extensive processing while others are treated more perfunctorily. In sport no single cue demands the focus of your attention for extended periods of time. While your attention is selective, what is being selected may change rapidly from one moment to another. In a dynamic sport where there is an opponent (or opponents), selecting the proper course of action from several possible options is an ongoing process. Consider for a moment, if you will, all the information that is available to your awareness during performance. Much of this information originates in the environment but other information and cues originate within you. The focus of attention on the self, as compared to the environment, will have different experiential and behavioral consequences in sport. As the attention focus increases on what is going on around you in sport, the attention to the self will diminish. Conversely, if the focus of attention is on the self, that is, on how worried you are about your performance in sport, then the attention to what is going on around you will diminish. This is perhaps the main cause of the lack of concentration so frequently observed in sport. You need to learn how to shift your attention from the self to the sport environment as the situation may demand. This ability to shift is more critical in some sports than in others. As an example, an open-skilled, dynamic sport will require more shifting of attention from self to environment than will a closed skill such as rifle shooting.

In sport, the environmental focus includes the immediate processing of information being picked up by the eyes and ears. The self-focus includes such things as the pounding of the heart, increased breathing rate, muscular tremor, and other manifestations of worry or anxiety about your performance. Many athletes discuss their nervousness (self-focus) before the competition;

however, most of them say they are not aware of these cues once they have begun to play. In essence, they have allowed their attention to be shifted away from the self to the cues now available in the environment. Others do not have the ability to shift as easily and take time to "adjust" to the game. Another classic example of the inability to shift from self back to the environment is when you make a mistake and continue to berate and degrade yourself well beyond the time of the mistake. You may lose several minutes of concentration and of play due to the inability to shift back to what is going on in the game. Others appear unable to shift at all and must be substituted for immediately after making a mistake. You need to learn to dismiss the self-focus after a mistake and to shift your attention immediately to what is happening and about to happen as opposed to what has already happened.

The components of sport increase the demand for environmental focus. First, the general rapid pace inherent in most open-skilled sports requires your attention to keep abreast of what is going on in the environment. Secondly, the ever-changing, unpredictable nature of most sports requires that your attention be directed outward to follow the development of the play. At the same time, sports offers many opportunities to increase the self-directed focus of attention as well. What is being experienced bodily is always vying for attention to the self. Physical effort in sport performance, the perception of pain, the emotional component of effort in performance who is watching you, preoccupation with a mistake you just made and so on are all conducive to shifting the focus of attention from the environment to the self. When the shift from environment to self is stimulated by any one arousal factor, it generally gravitates to other aspects of the self. This results in loss of concentration in sport.

Another factor in sport environments that is conducive to the shifting of attention from the environment to the self is the presence of spectators. The fact that the presence of an audience enhances self-focus is a factor that must be accommodated in the training of athletes. When you are concerned about what other people such as parents, coaches, or special friends think of your performance, it is difficult to keep your attentional focus on what you are doing.

In most sports, the ability to shift attention back and forth between the environment and the self is essential. Certain situations or cues in sport will predictably lead to shifts one way or another. Since you determine what stimuli you will attend to, there will be variations in attentional focus. However, there is some evidence to support the fact that you can learn how to focus your attention and how to shift in the necessary direction or to reshift when cues have automatically created a shift that is not conducive to maximizing performance at that given moment in time. It should be emphasized that in most sports a shift to self-focus interferes with performance.

Where and When to Focus Attention

Focusing on the components of well-learned behavior disrupts the performance. At the same time, focusing on the elements of a poorly learned activity or one that is just being learned is facilitative or even essential to the performance. This leads to the question of why would the focus of attention in one case be facilitative to performance and, in the other case, be disruptive?

Focusing on the components of the performance slows the behavior down in such a manner that smoothness, the coordination of the whole, or the flow of the act, is disrupted. As an example, if either a typist or a musician focuses on what the fingers are doing, they cannot execute the performance as smoothly or as effectively as when their focus is on a level of performance that is superordinate to the action of the fingers. It is the higher-order systems in sport performance that are responsible for the sense of sequence and smoothness of performance. In sport, you can easily disrupt a smooth execution of a skill by focusing on what you are doing. As an example, if you have an exceptional jump shot and have been asked to demonstrate it to other athletes, the execution will deteriorate as you are asked to focus on the position of the hand, the snap of the wrist, the follow through, etc. Performance becomes disjointed when you focus on component parts. You have to focus on what is about to happen, then just let it happen!

On the other hand, focus on the elements or component parts of a skill is facilitative, even necessary for some, to the learning of the overall organization of the act. This type of attentional focus produces a more careful selection of appropriate component acts and a more thorough monitoring of the execution of them than would otherwise occur. This approach allows for adjusting and smoothing as it develops and organizes the sequence of acts to a coordinated whole. Consciously attending to the sequence of acts leads to a gradual assumption of automaticity in the execution. This is the goal of learning every athletic skill in such a way that it is executed at a level that does not require your attentional focus, freeing the attention so that it can be directed to what is about to happen in the game.

Attention and Maximizing Performance

When athletes enjoy what they are doing, they report specific changes in their attentional processing. They report that they narrow their attention so that it is focused exclusively on the task at hand. This is what we call "concentration." This focused attention is the prerequisite for maximal performance or working at the peak of your capacity at whatever you are doing. It is certainly essential for maximizing your performance in sport.

Maximal sport performance occurs when intense concentration of attention is focused on a limited stimulus field. In other words, the athlete must be able to select the relevant cues from the multitude available and focus solely on them. All irrelevant stimuli are eliminated, shut off, or ignored.

Peak performance occurs when you voluntarily concentrate on the cues in the environment and perceive them to demand an action that is within your ability to execute. In other words, the challenge of the situation must match your perceived ability in order to maintain the concentration throughout the execution. If there is an imbalance between the challenge and the skills, attention will waver. That is, if your opponent is much more skilled, concentration will lapse. Or, if you are much more skilled than the opponent, concentration will lapse. This explains the classical upsets that occur in sport season after season. The relationship between the balance of the challenge and skills and sustained concentration has been observed not only in sport but in many other leisure and/or occupational pursuits.

Attention is the means by which you pick up and exchange information from the sports environment. When this process is under your control, you feel you can direct the flow or reciprocal information that unites you with the environment and what is going on within the game. You choose to interact with a system of continuous stimuli which you can modify and from which you can get meaningful feedback. You know they matter, that they are part of something you can control. This ability to focus attention is the most basic way of reducing anxiety about performance, and about what others think, or to refocus after a mistake or lapse in concentration.

Maximal performance is based on acquiring the skills and

Focusing attention is to become aware of only one thing or one area.

discipline to execute the behaviors that are demanded within the situation. Developing these abilities requires extensive commitment of attention to learn and to practice so they can be applied when demanded. Any maximal performance in sport requires concentrated attention to the exclusion of all other stimuli that become irrelevant in the situation. Outstanding accomplishment in sport requires concentration as any scientific, artistic, or creative effort does. Maximal performance depends on acquiring, recombining, adjusting, and producing behaviors. Hence, concentration is an inevitable prerequisite.

Only when you choose to pursue sport will you be motivated to sustain concentration long enough to produce superior performance. You can be forced to perform, however, attention cannot be controlled by external manipulation. Learning to become responsible for your own concentration is essential for maximal performance. Total involvement or total concentration in terms of how the attention is directed, where it is directed, and who is in control of the process, must be your responsibility.

Types of Attentional Focus

Focusing attention is becoming aware of only one thing or one area. It may involve a sense of slowing down what is really happening or of seeing it larger than real life. Certain positions in specific sports or certain types of sports require one type of attentional focus, while other positions and sports require a different type. A narrow focus of attention, that is, looking at one thing or a relatively small area, is required in target sports, in shooting sports, in basketball shooting, in kicking a field goal or an extra point. A broad focus is needed for most team games where you have to be aware of your opponents as well as your teammates, and in specific positions such as quarterback or mid-fielder. Further, most team sports require the ability to shift from broad to narrow and back to broad, whereas most closed skills demand a narrow focus of attention throughout the task. Team sport athletes need to learn to adjust and change their focus of attention much as a zoom lens on a camera or a spotlight on stage zooming in on a specific point.

Frequently you may have the necessary skills and strategies, but lack the ability to make proper application of them in a game situation. The challenge becomes one of "freeing" your body and brain, of letting it happen. You will need to learn to relax, to get rid of all of the nonessentials, so that concentration can occur. When you sense pressure, the focus of attention is on outside factors, such as being aware of the coach, the spectators, judges, or significant others who have expectancies for the performance. An athlete who is relaxed and confident can just let it happen, blocking out everything except relevant cues.

Another classification of attentional focus involves the distinction between an internal focus and an external focus. The internal focus is basically the self-focus that has been discussed previously. This involves focusing on how you feel, what is happening to your body, being concerned about what others think about your performance, etc. Obviously, the attention is not directed to what is going on in the sport environment. External focus is directing the attention focus toward the task, or the game that is underway or about to begin. In some sports, an internal focus is desired. In other sports, the ability to shift from an internal to an external focus and back again is necessary. As an example, the ability to pace yourself in a swimming or running race requires the ability to monitor your physiological demands in such a way that you do not go out too fast or start the "kick" too soon. When swimmers and runners have the ability to judge their splits and times to the second, they obviously have the ability to switch from internal to external focus and to monitor both with precision. In much the same manner, a marathon runner needs to be able to monitor both external and internal factors and to switch back and forth so as to avoid getting into difficulty by not pacing properly, not taking in sufficient fluids, or not paying attention to pain.

There has been much discussion about association and dissociation in terms of what one is paying attention to during a performance. This has been used in reference to endurance sports such as swimming or running, as well as a way of coping with discomfort or pain. Association is much like self-focus or internal focus, while dissociation is similar to environmental or external focus. Basically, association is focusing on what is happening to your body and your thoughts are directed toward things that involve the self. Dissociation, on the other hand, can involve a focus on external concerns or be specifically directed toward turning the attention away from the self. As an example, in sports requiring endurance, such as marathon running, the athlete may follow a particular thought pattern to get his/her attention away from the discomfort of running. Or, in the case of pain, focusing the attention away from the pain to thoughts that are pleasurable or enjoyable would be considered to be dissociation.

Variations in Concentration

As mentioned previously, the intensity and the duration of the attentional focus can vary considerably. Individuals differ in their ability to control both intensity and duration and still manage to perform at an exceptionally high level. As an example, Jack Nicklaus generally maintains intense concentration throughout a golf match and appears to be aloof from the spectators. Lee Trevino, on the other hand, is able to maintain intense concentration until the ball is hit and then shift his focus to the spectators and enjoy the crowd. He has the ability to shift back and forth, whereas Jack Nicklaus does not appear to have that ability. Another example of differences in concentration can be observed in tennis. Bjorn Borg and Chris Evert-Lloyd tend to maintain intense concentration throughout the match. Jimmy Connors and, more particularly, John McEnroe appear to have the ability to switch from the spectators, to arguing with the officials, to yelling at themselves, back to the game and continue to play at a high level of performance. The real question might be, how good would they be if they really concentrated throughout the match? It is possible that some personality types have different patterns of concentration. The important consideration is whether the switching back and forth, as opposed to maintaining concentration, interferes with your performance. If it does, then you need to work on developing strategies to help sustain concentration when other factors tend to disrupt it.

Some athletes have spoken of experiencing altered states of awareness or altered perceptions when they have had exceptional performances. They report shifts in alertness, of having sharpened vision, exceptional hearing and kinesthetic sensations of great clarity. They feel as though every movement energizes them for greater performance. All report that they feel more in touch with all senses and sensations; they register things that are usually missed without this heightened awareness in the normal course of participation. Following the performance, they have total recall of what happened in minute detail. Stan Musial said that when he had this great concentration and heightened awareness, he did not guess where a pitch would be, he KNEW! When he was concentrating at this intensity, he could always tell where and how the pitch would come to him.

The ability to be aware of everything that is going on within the game is necessary for maximal performance. The absence of worry about your performance is a prerequisite to allowing this intense concentration to occur, which, in turn, allows for maximal peripheral vision and the ability to pick up the relevant cues. Pele, the great soccer player, appeared to know exactly where everyone on the field was and what each was about to do when he played. Without question, some athletes are better at letting this type of intense concentration happen than others; however, everyone can improve through training and practice.

Mental Errors

Mental errors are generally caused by lack of attention or inattention or just laziness due to lack of motivation. If practices allows this type of inattention, then the performance will be much like the practice. The quality of the practice has to be such that the athletes are challenged to give their undivided attention throughout the practice. Far too many practices are boring, repetitious, and nonproductive, with athletes standing around waiting for instructions that take too long. If the quality of the practice is improved, less time is needed for practice, and the attention given to the practice by the athletes will be much more intense.

Mental errors are caused by anxiety, worry, and pressure. Under these conditions, athletes forget to do things since their attention is not on what they are doing. They end up trying too hard to compensate for their anxiety and worry about how they will do. They also tend to rush plays and rush their execution under these conditions. Confidence in one's ability prevents anxiety and allows the athlete the luxury of not rushing, of not making a move until the time is right. Concentration, attentional focus or task-oriented focus provides the condition to know when to make the move.

Coaches contribute greatly to situations which produce anxiety and pressure for the athletes. When they demand perfect execution, when they rant and rave at athletes, when they berate the athlete who does not perform to expectations, coaches create environments where the athlete's attention is directed away from maximizing performance. Coaches who use punishment and/or demeaning comments as motivation add further to the pressures that are already there.

Generally, coaches view mental errors as being different from physical ones. Somehow they have the notion that physical errors are part of the game and are expected to some degree. On the other hand, they feel that no one should make mental errors. Yet, mental and physical errors cannot be separated; both are caused by the situations which interfere with single-minded focus on the tasks at hand. Coaches and athletes need to accept the fact that they need to train for the mental skills with the same degree of regularity as the physical ones. In fact, the mental skills are more complicated and require more regular practice than the physical ones; however, the practice does not take as long as it does for the physical skills.

Learning How To Concentrate

You cannot concentrate on concentrating and accomplish very much. The real secret is to "just let it happen" at the conscious level. Begin by letting your thoughts drift wherever they wish and experience how that feels. Become aware of how one thought leads to another without any conscious direction on your part. Allow thoughts to zoom in and zoom out; practice broadening and narrowing them consciously. Experience what it feels like to focus on different kinds of thoughts. As an example, while running, think about stretch, float, glide, etc., and see if you can observe any difference in your running style. Become aware of different sensations of the body as you focus on self-attention. Again, do not concentrate on concentrating or try to do something the mind is not trained to do. You must practice these experiences consciously and practice "just letting it happen." Do not worry if the mind wanders because it will; just let the concentration lapse and then refocus and concentrate again without a struggle. The more times you practice this, the easier it will become and the fewer times you will experience a concentration lapse. It is essential to eliminate the constant strain to concentrate.

Practice concentrating on one thing at a time and trying to passively maintain the focus. Focusing on your breathing is a good exercise to practice as breathing is always with you. If it isn't, it won't matter anyway! Focus your attention by counting "one" as you inhale, and "two" as you exhale. If your mind wanders between breaths, just disregard it, let the thoughts pass on through, and come back to focusing on inhaling and exhaling. Keep the breathing relaxed; do not try to force or alter the regular breathing rhythm. Just learn to let it happen with a passive but conscious awareness of the process. When other thoughts intrude (as they most surely will), dismiss them, let them pass on through, and come back to attending to your breathing. With practice, you will discover that you can focus for a longer period of time without having your mind wander.

There are natural fluctuations in concentration. The more involved, motivated, and "tuned in" you are to what you are doing, the easier it is to learn to concentrate. In doing anything, if you are not focusing in one hundred percent, then you are not performing to your potential. You have to learn to think efficiently about your worries and concerns as they will always be there. It is better to learn to let them pass through and learn how to come back to focusing on what you are doing, rather than trying to ignore them or become occupied in some other way so they do not interrupt your performance. However, if you are not worried or anxious, then there are no distractions! There will be more discussion about how to reduce worry in the chapters on Relaxation and Self-thoughts.

Remember, the mind is a complex thing; information is being processed from all directions. All the combinations of what is going on, what one remembers and associates with what is going on, and what has happened in previous situations, are continuously being processed with such complexity that the brain makes an IBM computer look like a toy. Learning to get things together and categorized, connected, and integrated takes time. Learn to use things that work for you as you learn to free the body and brain to integrate, to "let it happen" without interference. Do not expect to revolutionize your attentional focus all at once. If learning these skills were that simple, everyone would be under self-regulatory control all the time! No athlete would ever make a mental error!

Raja Yoga, or mental yoga, is the science of concentration. Those who practice this yoga maintain that a progression of exercises improves concentration, enhances mental abilities, and develops a photographic memory. Concentration on breathing is basic to other steps of learning. Focusing of the attention is practiced in a very gentle, "just let it happen," procedure. This is always preceded by relaxation techniques. (See the chapter on Relaxation for more information.) Trying to force concentration is always counterproductive.

Specific exercises to increase concentration involve geometric patterns that you can make from construction paper. Some individuals frame theirs and have them available to use to refocus concentration when it lapses. In Eastern lore, these geometric patterns are called yantras. Basically, they provide the same cues for focusing attention on a non non-arousing stimulus as the mantra does in Transcendental Meditation™.

Practicing with Yantras

Place a yantra that consists of a black background approximately
12″ × 12″ with a white 2″ square glued in the exact center on a
white wall at eye level. Sit about 3 feet away and get into a relaxed
state. Close your eyes for a few minutes while picturing in your
mind's eye a black, velvety smooth screen. If other images come
into your mind's eye, just let them pass on through and come
back to seeing the black velvet background.

Once you can see the black background without effort, open
your eyes and passively look at the white square on the black
background in front of you. Continue looking at it without effort
until you can see an edge of color forming around the white
square. When this happens, gently move your gaze to the white
wall where an after-image will appear. You may have a negative,
that is a white background with a black square, as your after-
image. Continue to hold this after-image as long as you can.
When it begins to fade, try to imagine that it is still there. Repeat
the exercise again and continue to practice it a couple of times
each day for a week. This exercise will help you improve your
concentration and to learn how to transfer images viewed in the
mind's eye and to regenerate them when they fade away. This is
basic to learning how to use imagery in improving performance.
(See the chapter on Imagery.)

Another yantra can be made on the flip side of the black background by placing a bright yellow circle approximately four
inches in diameter in the center of the black square. Attach this to
the wall at eye level and get in a relaxed state. Close the eyes and
imagine the black, velvety screen. Open your eyes gently and
focus without effort on the yellow circle. Now imagine it is a spotlight that is coming closer and closer to you until it completely fills
the black background. Now let it zoom away from you until you
see only a pinpoint of light, then the black background again.
Practice this exercise several times a day until you can complete
it in the mind's eye without the stimulus of the yantra. Practice
changing the color of the circle in your mind's eye, as well as
changing the pattern of motion by having the circle rotate and
change into another color as it turns. Learning to alter the size, the
color, and the motion of a yantra is basic to being able to learn
how to use concentration and imagery to practice sport skills.
(See the chapter on Imagery for more information.)

Additional Concentration Exercises

From the basic exercises, you can move to others that add more dimension and incorporate more mind/body links. As an example, sit in a relaxed state, close your eyes, and imagine a black velvety screen for a few minutes. Now, in the mind's eye, concentrate on an orange. Experience it in as many ways as you can. In the mind's eye, pick it up, see the color, smell the fruit, peel it and eat it if you like oranges. Become aware of how your imagination influences your bodily responses. Are you aware of the oil of the orange skin on your hands, of the stickiness? Can you smell the orange? Do you begin to salivate at the thought of eating it?

Another exercise which begins to get closer to your sport consists of examining carefully in the mind's eye a piece of athletic equipment, an athletic shoe, a running shoe, or a part of your uniform. Again, get into a relaxed state, close your eyes, and begin to examine the object in your mind's eye. In a group practice, if the athletes are all involved in the same sport, it is better to provide them with the object they are to examine in their mind's eye. As an example, if they are all runners, have them examine their running shoes. They should see the colors, the trademarks, the scuff marks, the way it is worn, the laces, the sole, and the inside. Examine it from all perspectives. Have them discuss their experience in concentrating on their shoe. Some may have "put them on" and/or imagined they were running in them. If this happens, have them re-experience the concentration exercise and keep the image a static one. This teaches control of the concentration which is essential if imagery exercises are to be practiced and learned. You must learn to concentrate on specific items and not let your concentration wander wherever it wishes.

There is no limit to the types of exercises that can be created to assist in teaching concentration and focusing of the mind. They should be applicable to the sport situation that is familiar to the athlete. The coach can provide the leadership and direct the exercises. However, you should be encouraged to develop your own exercises and to practice them on your own, off and on during the day. You should not spend too long on these exercises at one time. Five minutes at a time will usually suffice and noticeable improvement will be observed in a few weeks time. If you have difficulty in seeing color, continue practicing in a passive manner. Trying too hard will prevent it from happening. If you dream in color, you should be able to see color in your mind's eye with continued relaxed practice.

An exercise that demonstrates how mental concentration influences muscular response is another one that athletes enjoy doing. It is also a good topic of conversation in social situations where it can be practiced as well. Using a string approximately ten inches long, attach a key, ring, or some other small weight so that it becomes a small plumb line. Stabilize the elbow of the dominant arm on a desk or table while holding the string gently between the thumb and forefinger of the dominant hand with the hand and forearm elevated to a 45° angle. Get into a comfortable, relaxed state and focus your attention on the weight at the end of the string. Concentrate on that weight moving in a clockwise circle. Just let it happen. You will notice that the weight begins to move in that pattern without any observable, overt movement of the hand or arms. This exercise demonstrates quite easily and obviously how you think with your muscles. As a matter of fact, you cannot think without your muscles responding at some level. This fact explains why mental concentration on skill performance helps you learn a skill, improve, or perfect the execution of a skill. (See the chapter on Imagery for more information.)

The string exercise can include practice in a counterclockwise pattern, as well as a pendulum pattern away from the body and back, or back and forth parallel to the shoulders. Practice all of these patterns. You will notice that you may have very tight, precise patterns of movement during this exercise, while others may have a wider, free-swinging motion. These individual differences can be acknowledged; however, they make no difference in terms of the skill being learned. See the chapter, "Monitoring Your Progress" for more specific directions.

The Grid Exercise has been used rather extensively in the Eastern Bloc countries with athletes. It is reported that athletes are selected for competition immediately prior to the event by their performance on this task. Basically, the exercise tests the athlete's level of concentration at that point in time. If an athlete is worried, anxious, or distracted by interrupting thoughts, the concentration is lessened. In skills where concentration is absolutely essential to good performance, such as gymnastics, figure skating, or shooting, this exercise may serve as a guide for selecting those who are able to concentrate the best. The Grid Exercise for a team is as follows: Hand out a form of the Grid, face down, to the athletes. Before they turn the Grid over to look at it, tell them that they are to put a slash mark through numbers in numerical sequence starting with Number 11. They will have one minute to get as many as they can. You will start them with a signal, "Begin," and stop them at the end of one minute. Athletes who have the ability to really concentrate, scan, and store relevant cues will usually score in the upper 20s and into the 30s in terms of the numbers they will find in sequence. Those who cannot concentrate, that is, cannot disregard everything except the task at hand will score much lower.

You will note that you can use the same form several times, especially if they do not score very high as they are beginning to learn how to concentrate. With the second instruction have them begin with Number 33 and go as high as they can. The third time, you can have them begin with 66 or some other number that no one has reached in previous exercises. Several forms of the Grid can be developed to change the location of the numbers. The only requirement is that all numbers be 2 digit ones and that they are arranged in a fashion similar to a bingo card. See chapter, Monitoring Your Progress for a sample Grid.

Another advantage of this exercise is that of creating differing situations while the athletes are doing the exercises. You can talk throughout the session, play music, make noise, chew gum loudly, or whatever, to attempt to distract them and break their concentration. As concentration improves, they learn to block out everything and concentrate fully on the task at hand. This exercise can be used to compare performance in a non-stressful situation with that just before the contest to see if the athletes learn to control their anxiety and to focus their attention on the task at hand regardless of the situation. Ideally, that is the skill that you are trying to teach the athletes.

In summary, if you can develop concentration skills and strategies which are prepotent over your worry, then you can develop consistent performance. The difference between the best performance and the worst performance lies within the ability to concentrate, to shift your attentional focus, and to disregard irrelevant cues. Practice of these concentration exercises on a regular basis will provide the skills and strategies needed to focus in a single-minded fashion on the task at hand without distraction or disruption. If you can learn to focus your attention on what you are about to do, it is impossible to worry at the same time. Preoccupation with worry raises anxiety and takes away concentration. Anxiety is always dysfunctional to performance.

5

CREATING YOUR OWN INSTANT REPLAYS OF PERFORMANCE

Most of us daydream and re-experience situations in our imagination in a haphazard manner. The fact that we can remember previous experiences in a rather detailed fashion is why imagery, visualization, mental rehearsal or mental practice works for athletes. Virtually all good athletes have discovered this technique on their own and use imagery to improve their learning and performance of sports skills. For full benefit, it is important to learn how to control imagery rather than let it wander as thoughts pass in and out of our mind in a daydreaming fashion.

Barbara Brown, in her book, *Supermind*, discussed imagination as the ultimate energy. She said that imagination was the most neglected and underdeveloped ability of humans. All of us have this ability to create and re-create pictures of things and events in our mind's eye even though they occurred at some other time and place, however, it is a little understood resource. Almost nothing is known about the process of imagining and how to develop it into a strategy that can be utilized to improve performance and well-being of humans. According to Brown, imagination can re-create the past in great detail or transform it to fit the emotional states desired. It can project into the future, solve problems, gain relief from mental pressures, assist in learning and maximizing performance, and entertain us. In short, visualizing in your mind's eye is a powerful tool that you can use to improve anything and everything that you do. You can gain greater control over your body, your emotions, and your concentration, and integrate them all in a fine-tuned fashion to maximize your potential in whatever you pursue. Using imagery in sport is of particular importance because you literally "think with your muscles." As you learn to control your imagery in your mind's eye, your muscles gain greater control as well. More about that later.

Many athletes use imagery to improve their performance, however, few have been given instruction and guidance in ways to gain all the potential that mental practice might offer. Jack Nicklaus said that hitting a good golf shot combines ten percent swing, forty percent stance and setup and fifty percent consists of the mental picture one has of how the swing should occur. He talks of "movies in his head" when he plays and says that he never hits a shot, not even in practice, without having an in-focus picture of how it will occur.

Dwight Stones pictures his high jump in his mind's eye before he takes off on the approach. Weight lifters execute their lift mentally before the actual attempt. O. J. Simpson ran plays in his head over and over so that when the play was called in a game he was ready. Fran Tarkenton visualized everything involved while running entire blocks of plays in his head. He tried to visualize every game situation, every defense the opposing team could setup, and what he would do in each and every situation he could imagine. Chris Evert–Lloyd carefully rehearses every detail of her anticipated match including her opponent's style, strategy, what she will do if this happens, if that happens, and so on. Almost without exception, superior athletes utilize their imagination abilities to prepare for their performance.

What Is Imagery?

You will find that several terms are used to explain what is basically the same process. This process involves recalling from memory pieces of information stored there from all types of experiences and reshaping them into a meaningful reverie via a thought process. Inasmuch as experiences can be remembered through several sense organs, you may be able to see, to taste, to experience sound, to feel texture, speed, and other sensory stimuli kinesthetically, depending on what you are re-experiencing in your mind's eye. Many athletes do not "see" as such in their mind's eye; their mental images are not visual. Instead, they may be experiencing kinesthetically muscular responses. They actually "feel" themselves doing what they are imagining. Other dimensions of the re-experience may involve emotional reactions, sensations of touch, sound, or combinations of any of these.

When most athletes think of mental practice or mental rehearsal, they usually think it involves watching a movie of themselves executing their sport skills. Some even discuss different types of imagery in terms of how they "see" when they use mental imagery. One of these is called external imagery and is considered to be outside of you, like watching a movie or a videotape of your performance. Internal imagery is from inside you and considered to be rehearsing what you actually see with your own eyes when you execute your skills. As an example, if you were a figure skater, you would see everything around you as you would in the process of completing your routine. You would not see yourself as though you were watching a movie. Instead, it would be like a camera on your head taking pictures of all the things you would see as you skate.

Yet a third type of mental imagery is that of not actually seeing anything in your mind's eye but "experiencing" it or "feeling" it kinesthetically. In the final analysis, it does not matter which of these you use if it works for you!

The different types of mental rehearsal may be related to the degree to which you have learned a skill. That is, if you are just learning a new skill, you may find that external imagery works best. That is why it helps to see someone else do the skill or to watch a film of someone demonstrating the skill. Once you know what it is you are to do, you can see yourself executing the skill just as you watched others. As you learn the skill you may find that you begin to internalize it. You see the environment in which you perform and how that changes as you execute your skill. Finally, when you have learned it well, you may not see anything; you may only "feel" your way through as you use mental practice. That is, you imagine with your muscle sense, not visual sense. "You think with your muscles."

Imagery has been distinguished from mental practice or rehearsal in that imagery involves the ability to passively develop an image without going beyond that point. By comparison, rehearsal is being actively involved in an image or a series of images. It might be that one needs to learn how to hold an image before mental rehearsal can reach its potential in improving performance. Obviously, if you cannot hold an image, it will be difficult to control a series of them. Most all sports involve a series of dynamic and ever changing images and situations. The better the development of your bodily sensations and awareness, the more visual and kinesthetic cues you will have to incorporate in your mental rehearsal of the activity. Begin to notice what form your imagery takes so that you can concentrate on becoming more aware of these cues. Is it mainly kinesthetic, visual, or auditory?

Do you see things in color or black and white? If you dream in color you should be able to imagine in color. Do you see/feel things as an active participant or do you watch as though removed from the activity?

Some athletes have distinguished mental rehearsal from mental imagery by observing that they tend to just think about the task when told to mentally rehearse it. As an example, when told to mentally rehearse shooting a foul shot in basketball, they just thought about shooting it. On the other hand, when told to use mental imagery in shooting a basket, they imagined themselves actually shooting the foul shot. This distinction may be immaterial to the process of using your imagination, however, if you find just thinking about it does not incorporate as much sensory involvement as imagining you are executing it, then by all means, use your imagination.

It does appear that you must utilize "pictures" in your imagination as opposed to verbal descriptions. To mentally imagine a sequence of events you do not have time to decribe them and imagine they are occurring at the tempo they must be executed. For this reason, it is important that you learn to see, feel and experience through images rather than word descriptions. Practice in seeing images, in seeing color, and in being able to control the pictures in your mind's eye become important skills to develop. In short, mental imagery involves experiencing everything, all aspects, all dimensions, in a holistic total experience. In the final analysis, it does not matter whether you call it mental imagery, mental practice, mental rehearsal, visualization, or whatever. The important thing is to learn to include all dimensions involved in the situation and to incorporate all your senses in experiencing performance in your mind's eye.

Imagery needs to be individualized so you will have to learn to read your own cues and utilize those that are most effective for you. You, and only you, can determine how you perceive situations and store cues that allow you to re-experience the situation again and again, totally removed from when and where it occurred. That indeed, is the stuff of which memories are made and memories allow you to come back to your mind's eye again and again to relive the situations that you have recorded there.

Benefits of Imagery
Knowing everything there is to know about mental imagery, visualization, mental practice, or mental rehearsal will not contribute

to improving your performance unless you practice and work with the skills and strategies on a regular basis. Becoming more aware of all dimensions of your experience while performing is essential and provides the necessary cues to include in your mental rehearsal. Because we literally "think with our muscles" we need to become aware of these feelings. Our body is literal, that is, it cannot always distinguish among the stored memories whether we have just thought about doing something or whether we have actually done it. How many times have you had your memory jogged in such a way that it brings a clear image in focus, however, you cannot determine whether you dreamed about it, just thought about it, or actually experienced it! This inability of the mind/body connection to distinguish what you have thought about, dreamed about, or actually performed is one of the great benefits of mental imagery. If you can learn to think about something in a systematic and detailed fashion, it becomes a part of you. Your body just knows it has been there before. The more often you can imagine what you have done and/or wish to do, the more familiar it becomes. Your body does not always know how or when it was experienced, it just knows that it has been there before—deja vu.

The deja vu effect occurs because we cannot think or imagine without some level of physical response. When an action is imagined the central nervous system sends impulses in a pattern associated with that action. The stimulation that originated cognitively (by imagining) is manifested bodily in the neurological patterns generating low levels of muscular response. The more you practice this, the more efficient and effective subsequent imagery or action becomes. Using this strategy, you can practice what you have already learned in order to improve your performance or you can increase the speed of your learning by adding these additonal mental practices. Many gymnasts have had the experience of not being able to execute a new trick or a greater degree of difficulty in a routine when they leave the practice session. The next day when they return to practice, after thinking about it off and on during the course of the day, they discover they can execute the trick. Knowing what you are trying to do and then imagining that you are doing it is a very good way to improve your performance without any physical practice. Athletes who have been too tired to continue physical practice have been able to use mental practice and continue making progress in their skill acquisition. Other athletes have maintained their skill during injury and rehabilitation using mental imagery.

Brown, in her book, *Supermind*, indicated there were two remarkable benefits of imagery that have been scientifically validated but not systematically used to increase human performance. First, the more specific and detailed the image, the more specific the effect. That is, cognitively you can excite and generate impulses that are specific to the pattern of response necessary to produce the movement. Secondly, imagining makes the body work; mental images direct and activate the neurological patterning of nerve to make the body respond exactly the way the image directs it. This effect has tremendous implications for athletes. The effect of mental imagery causes an expenditure of energy due to the neural and muscular response that occurs when you imagine movement. You think with your muscles! If you concentrate and imagine you are executing your sport skill just as you would like, you are not ony imagining; you are preparing your body to perform. Your nerves, muscles, heart, breathing, and sympathetic nervous system all intregrate with the initial cognitive image to see/feel yourself accomplishing your designated performance.

The optimal level of arousal can also be generated via imagery. You can either increase your arousal or decrease it with imagery. Obviously, you will need to learn how to read your bodily cues to determine what your reference point is for optimal arousal. Imagery enhances self-regulatory skills, self-awareness, self-assessment, self-control and the ability to read your cognitive and somatic cues under all contitions.

Another positive benefit of imagery is being able to imagine situations and practice all types of options in sports performance that you cannot possibly setup in practice. Some sports and some positions in specific sports lend themselves to this type of practice. As an example, if you have no way of practicing against someone who is better than you, you can imagine you are competing against an opponent who has a higher skill level. Or, as a goalie, you may not be able to have your teammates shoot every type of shot at you but you can "practice" stopping those in your head. If you feel that you did not get the specifics that you needed in your practice, or that certain skills that you need were not included in practice, these can be performed in your head. In fact, you can practice anything in your head and prepare in a manner that may not always be possible in physical practice. Many times when the physical practice seems to be going nowhere, the solution is to try mental practice to assist in getting off the plateau. You can setup all types of conditions and situations in your head with mental imagery that you cannot possibly structure in a real life practice.

Imagery can improve the coordination and precision of your execution by increasing awareness of body position, amount of force, intensity of effort, or any other dimension of your performance. Accurate analysis of skill execution and stategy can also be experienced through imagery. You can use imagery to correct mistakes, and to change bad habits as well as improve skill production. Imagery has also been used to speed up recovery from fatigue. This is of particular importance in sports that extend over a long period of time or in those where competition continues over a period of days such as track and field or fencing.

You can use imagery to "psych up" prior to a competition and to maintain motivation throughout practice or competition. Imagery can also be used to decrease worry and anxiety about your performance and to increase your enjoyment of performance under any conditions. You can change beliefs, attitudes, and memories of previous performances through imagery and learn to produce the positive imagery necessary to execute without disruption. You can also generate energy through imagery. If you are a marathon runner and begin to tire, you can use imagery to "recharge" and continue. The same approach holds true for any endurance sport.

Mental imagery practice is generally more effective with the highly skilled athlete, however it can be used at any skill level. The more you know about what you are imagining, the more effective the practice. Imagery is easier to practice in those sports where the execution of the skills takes place in similar and controlled situations. Individual sports are more conducive to imagery practice because they are less complex. That is, you have more control of the situation than in a team sport where you have to react to ever-changing situations and opponents. Individual sports which do not involve anyone else such as gymnastics, diving, skating, and the like lend themselves to mental imagery practice better than individual sports such as tennis and other racquet sports where you are reacting to an opponent.

Team sports involve many additional dimensions but can be practiced in your mind's eye as well. For instance, imagery can be used to practice specific plays or specific offenses or defenses. In addition, if you are having difficulties executing a skill such as a certain type of pass, you can use imagery for increased practice. Mental practice in combination with physical practice provides the best method of preparation for competition. Mental rehearsal is not a substitute for physical practice, however, it can enhance both the amount and the quality of practice.

Using Mental Imagery

Mental imagery is not daydreaming about the great athlete you would like to be! Nor is it wishful thinking about how you would like to perform. It is a learned skill that requires effort, concentration, and discipline to acquire. A great deal of practice is needed to realize the full potential of this skill. The following suggestions will be helpful to you in knowing how to practice, when to practice, and how to apply imagery skills to situations in sport in order to help you maximize your performance.

Learning and Practicing Skills

- The skill, routine or sequence of movements should be rehearsed just as you would like to execute it. If you were rehearsing a dive, you would include climbing up on the board, the approach, hurdle, take-off, the planned dive, entry, and swimming back to the ladder to get out of the pool. All of the related and component parts of the skill should be rehearsed mentally at the same rhythm and tempo that you would like in your actual execution. This is important because the neurological pattern established through imagery should be exactly the same pace as needed for the actual performance. Doing things in slow motion in mental rehearsal can create errors in the actual execution. On the other hand, when learning a new skill, slowing down the imagery may be of some help in learning but only until the skill is learned.
- Use all the dimensions of the performance and as many cues as you can in preparing with mental rehearsal. The more of these you can incorporate, the more effective your imagery will be. Further, the more unknowns you can reduce about every detail and dimension that you think you might encounter in the performance, the better prepared you are! Try to include smells, sounds, and to visualize the environment, as well as the appropriate kinesthetic or feeling cues such as sensations of speed, tempo, coordination, and proprioceptive sensations of touch, pressure, and so on.
- The mental rehearsal should be successful, not perfect! If you

always imagine you execute everything perfectly, you set yourself up for sure failure most of the time. However, in closed skills such as archery, shooting, etc. you should imaging hitting the target, making the shot, or completing the task. you should imagine that you are performing equal to or better than your previous best performance. In this way you can always leave room for improvement. You have to learn to practice only successful images. If you have made a mistake in a recent performance, you need to re-play that competition in your head over and over until you see/feel yourself getting through that competition the way you would have liked. In this way you can always have an instant replay to correct and remove memories of errors. You must make sure that your rehearsal is realistic and within your reach. Goal setting and imagery go hand in hand in your mental preparation.

- You should use mental imagery in preparation for practice sessions as well as competition. Most of the mental practice should take place in preparation, however, whenever possible a mental rehearsal of what is about to happen will be beneficial. In some sports you have to do all of the mental preparation prior to competition as the time frame of the sport does not allow you to practice once the event has started. In a sport such as fencing, you have no time to rehearse on the strip. Diving, on the other hand, allows you time before your performance. Some team sports will provide breaks that allow time for mental practice while others do not. You will have to evaluate your particular sport and/or position to determine how you can best incorporate mental rehearsal. If the sport that you play allows you time to re-experience in your mind's eye how you would like to have executed a task immediately after committing an error, take the time to do it at that point. Practice until you complete the task the way you want it to be executed.

- Athletes who can pace themselves so well that they can call out their splits and times during races in running or swimming have learned to do this through imagery as well by becoming aware of how they feel at the pace they wish to set and then imagining in their mind's eye over and over. If you practice this, you learn more quickly how to evaluate your performance and how to imagine performing at the level you desire. It is important to utilize time as a marker in practicing your imagery. As you practice in your mind's eye, use a watch to see if you are rehearsing at the pace you wish to perform. As an example, if you wish to run a six-minute mile on a course that is familiar to you, can you mentally rehearse every detail of how you would run that race so that your imagery lasts exactly six minutes? You will have to establish time markers for your own particular sport so you can determine if your imagery is too slow or too fast.

- If you concentrate intently on your imagery, you should be aware of physical responses that will mimic, at a lower level of intensity, those produced in the actual performance. This type of response has been demonstrated over and over in the laboratory using electrodes on the major muscles that are used to perform the skill you are mentally rehearsing. Individual variation is evident, some athletes are much more physically active during their mental rehearsal while others are less active. However, evidence of muscular involvement during the mental practice occurs in all athletes to some degree. You think with your muscles!

- If you have access to videotaping or filming, you can utilize this technique to develop your mental imagery. As an example, if you were filmed during a superior performance, you should view that several times. While viewing it you should try to verbalize what you were thinking and how you felt when you executed that performance. This will provide you with the necessary cues for mentally rehearsing every detail in preparation for producing future superior performances.

- Re-experiencing a successful performance as soon after it has occurred is perhaps the best way to establish the bodily association of how a peak performance feels. When you "program" your body with that reference point, it is easier to prepare mentally for future performances equal to or better than your previous ones.

- In general, mental imagery can be practiced anywhere at anytime. Musicians reportedly practice while they are traveling. Athletes can utilize travel time in the same manner. A rifle shooter who was delayed due to weather knew that he was going to miss his practice rounds. During his flight he mentally shot his practice rounds in his head. He systematically loaded his rifle and shot each of 200 shots in exactly the manner followed in competition. He arrived just in time for the competition and proceeded to shoot his best score!

Many athletes find that doing mental practice just before falling asleep is an effective time and place for rehearsal. If you are trained to relax and eliminate muscular tension at will, this may be a good time for practice. However, if you find that you get aroused with your mental rehearsal and then have difficulty falling asleep, then you should select some other time. Anytime you can sit quietly and shut out distractions you can practice mentally. One big advantage is that you can practice in very short periods of time. You should learn to make use of many time periods throughout your day so you can utilize them for mental practice of some part of your performance. A high jumper reported that she used to sit in class and visualize a spot on the wall that was equal to the height she wished to reach and mentally jumped when the lectures got boring. While this might not be the best procedure, it does indicate how one can find time to practice! As was mentioned earlier, if your sport allows an opportunity for mental rehearsal immediately prior to performance, take advantage of that.

- Whether you practice mental imagery while sitting still or lying down or while "walking through" is a matter of preference and convenience. Many athletes can walk through or mimic whatever movements they execute when performing as they mentally rehearse what they are about to do. As an example, a diver may actually take the approach steps, hurdle, take-off and go through the basic bodily movements required in the dive while waiting for the next performance or turn. A gymnast can do the same thing while "on deck" for the upcoming event. You can determine when and how your sport allows you time for incorporating imagery and the type of imagery that you find most helpful in preparing for performance.

Imagery For and During Competition
- When you practice mentally you rehearse your entire performance under the competitive conditions you expect and the environment in which it is to take place. The more familiar you are with all details of the performance and the area where it is to occur, the better the mental rehearsal. If you are competing in a new environment you should try to get there before the competition so you can become familiar with it and incorporate it into your mental practice. When you cannot do that, pictures and films can sometimes provide the cues and establish enough familiarity so you can imagine that you are performing

there. This strategy was used with the U.S. Women's Field Hockey Team prior to a scheduled competition in Wembly Stadium in London to establish qualification for the 1980 Olympics. Since it was impossible for the athletes to visit Wembley Stadium or to practice there, the next best thing was to get a film of the U.S. Team playing England in Wembly Stadium some years earlier. This was done and the athletes watched the film with instructions to play close attention to the environment both visually and auditorily. Almost without exception the athletes said they felt as though they had been there before and were not overwhelmed by the nearly 70,000 spectators, the singing of English school girls, or the size of the stadium.

Another example of these techniques is that of a major football power in the collegiate circles. The players view films of their upcoming opponent and are instructed to pay close attention to details of the individual opponents they will face. Every cue and detail they can pick up from the film is processed in their memory. Colors, numbers, facial expressions, movement styles, and so on, along with the opponents' specific offensive and defensive plays and the general conditions under which they are called are all stored for future reference. The players are trained in relaxation techniques and the use of imagery so that they apply these cues to the projected competition. They are instructed to lie down, relax, and in their mind's eye, see/feel themselves facing their upcoming opponent and running the series of plays successfully they have been practicing all week. This team has traditionaly been one of the top collegiate teams over the years. Adding this dimension to their preparation may explain, in part, their continued success. This is yet another example of properly preparing a team for every dimension of the game. They do not encounter very many surprises in the real contest as they have, in a sense, "been there before." The more you can become familiar with the anticipated competition, the fewer unknowns and unexpected situations you will encounter. If the only unknown is the outcome of the contest, then all attention can be directed to that end. This should be your goal. You can devote all of your efforts to what is happening in the present and feel secure in having prepared properly for mentally processing all the cues and situations you anticipate in the competition.

• Strategies, set plays and specific responses can also be learned through mental imagery. if you are a third baseman on a baseball team, you can practice every conceivable double play in your mind's eye. As a goalie in any sport, you can prepare yourself for any type of an attack on goal by rehearsing mentally all the possible attempts on goal and see/feel yourself successfully defending each attack. Every sport can be broken down to parts which can be rehearsed mentally. In the final analysis, there is not anything that might occur in sport that cannot be mentally practiced in some way that will improve your reaction and response to it when it occurs during performance.

- Word cues and self-thoughts will assist you in focusing your imagery during performances. Again, this will vary from sport to sport, however you can devise ways to cue your concentration and focus for your particular sport. In gymnastics you can use words such as "stretch," "extend," "thrust," and so on as you perform which will help to produce the image you are trying to present. Some of you will find word cues work quite well. Others of you may discover that having a "picture" in your mind's eye of the type of presentation you wish to make during your performance may be more effective. You will have to experiment to discover which works best for you.

- Depending on the sport you play, you may have an opponent or teammate precede your performance. If, by chance, you observe them making a mistake or error, you should immediately focus on mentally seeing yourself complete that task without making mistakes. See yourself completing the task successfully. So often we see what appears to be a contagious response to making mistakes. You can prevent this by utilizing self-talk and mentally preparing, seeing/feeling yourself perform as you desire by blocking out any picture of a mistake being made.

- In preparing for whatever can occur during your performance, you can use mental imagery as well. For instance, if you are a skater, prepare yourself for recovery from a fall so you can get up and continue your routine. This is not to suggest that you rehearse falling, you only rehearse coping with that in the event it occurs. Gymnasts must do this so they are prepared if they happen to fall off a piece of the apparatus. Depending on your sport, you can prepare for any eventual happening using mental imagery. In most situations, mental imagery can prepare you for recovery from any unexpected occurrence. In this manner you can prepare for an immediate or anticipated problem that could conceivably occur. Continue to practice your routine from the point of interruption so you incorporate refocusing and developing confidence in all the skills that follow. If there is a specific difficult skill or part in your routine, a successful imagery after an error will be most helpful. See/feel yourself getting through the routine, skill, defense strategy, or whatever, continuing on at every point that an error or disruption of the plan might occur.

Recovery From Injury

• As mentioned previously, mental practice can be used while recovering from an injury or anytime that your practice has been prevented. Many athletes, while unable to perform, attend practice and go through everything mentally as they observe. Another effective technique that many have used to speed up recovery from injury or illness is to use visualization to increase blood supply to the injured area. Depending on the ability to concentrate, one can speed up recovery in this manner. Many of the Eastern Europeans reportedly utilize this strategy to recover from injury or from fatigue. You can practice such things as imagining your heart rate is slowing down and checking your pulse to see how effective you have become in altering that response. Others can increase or decrease the temperature in their fingers, or slow down their breathing rate. Try practicing these mentally and monitor your progress in learning to effect change in response to imagery. The Russians, in their applied psychology research, suggest that all of us can improve with practice, however, some are more successful in altering change in response than others. The practice of these skills should take place before you need them. That is, practice them so you will have them well learned if and when you need to use them. The same principle applies to learning to tolerate pain. As mentioned in the chapter on concentration, imagery is one of the most effective means of coping with pain. In your mind's eye, you can place yourself somewhere else, thus ignoring the situation in which you experience pain. While in the dentist's chair, you can imagine that you are in your favorite spot with people you enjoy. Or, while you are getting treatment for an athletic injury, you can, in your mind's eye, put yourself somewhere that you find pleasant and satisfying. In order to do this, you need to learn how to concentrate as well as hold an image in the face of real distraction!

These same principles are being used successfully in the treatment of many diseases and ailments. The medical field is now recognizing the value of a holistic approach to treatment and well-being. Terminal diseases such as cancer have been treated and gone into remission when patients have learned and utilized integration of mind and body to counter the disease. A disorder such as tinnitus or ringing in your ears can be coped with through skills of concentration and disassociation as well.

- When you practice imagery to cope with pain or to speed up recovery of disease, keep in mind that you can only concentrate on one thing at a time. As an example, if you have an athletic injury that is painful, you have to choose when you will focus mentally on reducing and coping with the pain and when you will imagine that blood flow is increasing in the area to speed up recovery. You will have to order your priorities; you can only use imagery for one thing at a time. The same holds true when using imagery in practicing any sport. You need to determine what it is you wish to accomplish first and work on that in your imagery. As mentioned previously, imagery and goal setting go hand in hand, so order your priorities or goals and work on them systematically.

In summary, mental imagery applied to sport performance is not a simple process. It is a skill that improves with practice. It is important that you learn the skills and strategies used with regular practice so you have them well learned when you need to apply them. Using them without prior practice does not work! You will be inclined to believe that imagery does not work in that case. You would never think of trying or practicing a skill only once and consider that you have learned it and understand it well enough to use it when you need it!

Skills of relaxation, concentration, self-thoughts, and goal setting strategies are also essential to the successful use of imagery. Each must be learned and practiced regularly to reach maximal performance potential. These skills and strategies are discussed at length in other sections of this book.

Steps to Becoming Proficient in Mental Imagery

As indicated previously, mental imagery is a skill that has to be practiced and learned. If you will read through the following exercises and practice them on a regular basis, you will learn to use imagery to improve your performance in sport. Keep in mind that these principles apply to anything that you might wish to accomplish so you can apply them in everyday situations beyond the sport environment. In each of these exercises, take a comfortable position with eyes closed. Spend only a few minutes with each one, repeating the exercises several times. You should observe improvement in a few weeks.

Exercise 1: Relaxing and Controlling Your Imagery

- As you become quiet and relaxed, focus on your breathing.
- Pay attention to bodily responses and sensations such as inhaling, exhaling, and the feeling of your body becoming warmer, heavier, and more relaxed with each breath.
- Notice any thoughts that come into your mind and try to let them pass on through without attending to them. Return to paying attention to your breathing.
- Take yourself from where you are and imagine that you are in your favorite place. This can be a beach, mountain, lake, or your own private spot that you retreat to for peace and comfort.

Exercise 2: Seeing Colors, Controlling and Changing

- In your mind's eye, visualize a spot of color such as red, zoom in until your whole visual field is covered with red, zoom out again until it recedes into blackness.
- Change the color to blue and repeat, continue this exercise using several colors. Each time start with a small dot of color, let it approach you like an oncoming light until it engulfs your entire visual field, then reverse direction until it disappears.
- This exercise will help you visualize color and to learn how to control movement.

Exercise 3: Controlling an Image, Learning to Keep the Mind Attending to an Image

- To improve your ability to maintain an image and observe detail, visualize your favorite athletic shoe.
- Examine every detail, the color markings, the scuff marks, wear and tear, lacings, or condition of the sole.
- Try to keep the imagery static, that is, do not let your mind wander to seeing/feeling yourself wearing it or running in it. If so, come back to seeing it in your hands as you examine it closely.

Exercise 4: Experiencing Tactile, Taste and Smell Through Imagery
- In your mind's eye, pick up a lemon. Feel the texture of the peeling, the oiliness.
- Smell the lemon, roll it on the table, take a bite out of the end and taste the juice.
- Note all the ways you can experience a lemon in your imagination.

Exercise 5: Experiencing Environmental Detail
- In your mind's eye, put yourself in your favorite room.
- Examine every detail you can imagine: furniture, color, texture, position, light and shadows, windows, and doors.

Exercise 6: Improving A Skill
- Select a specific skill or technique that you are currently trying to improve.
- See/feel yourself executing this skill better than you have ever done before.
- Repeat the mental rehearsal over and over, each time, performing it equal to or better than you have ever performed it before.
- Pay close attention to those aspects where you need work and make improvements in your mind's eye as you practice.
- If possible, after mentally rehearsing this skill, get to your physical practice. If you still have difficulty, return to your mental rehearsal. Your improvement will progress more rapidly when you combine mental practice with the actual physical practice in the same session.

Exercise 7: Dynamic Imagery, Putting It Into Action.
- Select some aspect of your sport. (If you play tennis, it can be the serve.) Use this example to develop your own strategy.
- See/feel yourself in your mind's eye executing the serve just as you desire and in a manner that is equal to or better than any serve you have ever delivered.
- In your ready position, see your opponent, see the service court, know where you plan to place the serve.
- See/feel yourself prepare for the toss, toss just where you desire, coordinate the preparatory movement with the racquet, and meet the ball at the point you desire.
- Follow through, see your serve go exactly to your target, see

your opponent return your service, see yourself return the ball setting it up for a put away on the next return.
- During this exercise, in whatever sport or part of a sport you select to mentally rehearse, make sure that you include the full and complete sequence of the movement to a point of completion, i.e., point declared, end of race, end of routine, etc. It is important to see/feel the aspect practiced from beginning to end.

Exercise 8: Eliminating Errors
- Select some aspect of your game or sport where you have been making an error during your performance.
- In your mind's eye, see/feel yourself executing the skill without the error just as you would like to perform.
- If the error persists in your mind's eye, imagine watching someone else who performs this skill correctly.
- Using this as a model in your imagination, see/feel yourself performing just as this person you have visualized performed the skill.
- Continue to practice this until you can repeat it over and over in your mind's eye without a mistake. Try to practice it physically as soon after this exercise as possible.

Exercise 9: Keeping a Performance Notebook
- One of the best exercises to increase your awareness and to develop cues for mentally rehearsing your previous best performances is to keep a notebook or diary.
- Record all cues regarding how you felt, what you thought about, how you prepared physically as well as mentally.
- Record the detailed procedures that you followed hours or even days prior to your best performance.
- Do this for practices as well as competitions.
- Peak performances or superior performances do not just happen! They occur because many factors that contribute to producing the performance come together. The only way to determine that pattern is to record everything leading up to it. Once you can establish a pattern of preparation, you can set the stage for the probability of it occurring again. It will not happen everytime, however, the probability of it occurring again is much better!

    The exercise of keeping a notebook will also provide you the opportunity of reviewing the progress you make in developing your mental skills for improving your performance. Some of these are so subtle that you will not notice any change unless you record your thoughts and feelings on a regular basis. You can go back and re-read your notes and chart your progress. This exercise fits nicely with the notion of goal setting. You can keep a record of short, immediate and long-term goals and integrate them into your imagery practice, or, use your imagery to see/feel yourself reaching your stated goals. See the chapter, "Monitoring Your Progress", for more details.

These exercises are just examples of how you can structure your imagery practice. As you become more proficient in this skill you will discover unlimited ways of practicing and preparing for every detail and aspect of whatever sport you play. You can begin to incorporate all the dynamic aspects of every sport, whether it be an individual, dual or team sport. You will learn to prepare for competitions by actually playing them in your head prior to the actual performance. In this manner, you can prepare for all possible occurrences. You will be able to experience in your mind's eye things that you may not have the opportunity to experience in real practice situations. This will be especially true when you do not have adequate competition to challenge you in your physical practice sessions. The first time you experience a deja vu that results from having been there before in your mind's eye, you will realize the great benefit of mental rehearsal in preparing for competition.

The objective of this type of preparation is to reach such a level of deja vu that you do not have to be concerned about anything in competitive situations except what is happening and about to happen in the game itself. Everything else will be there in such a way that you can "just let it happen." You will have prepared for every eventual occurrence that can conceivably happen and be able to "flow" with the game. The beautiful potential about using your imagination in sport is that it allows you to remember things of the past, to work on things in the present, and to project into the future in preparation for things that are yet to happen. It is one of the most effective ways of learning and improving skills and preparing for the application of them in dynamic settings. It is a skill which can be learned just like your physical performance skills.

6

SELF-TALK, SELF-THOUGHTS AND ATTITUDES

All of us, on many occasions, react with a wide range of behaviors and sometimes even opposite behaviors to situations and stimuli which are basically the same. It has been said many times that the only difference between the best performance and the worst performance is the variation in our self-talk and the self-thoughts and attitudes. Obviously, skill levels and physical states do not fluctuate widely within a game or between two performances over a short period of time. Variations in performing results from cognitive fluctuations.

Most of us, athletes included, go beyond what is occurring right here and now in our thought processing. Our awareness goes beyond what the situation is providing in that it triggers the memory of what has happened in the past in similar situations. We also tend to think about how that situation affected us, what we did about it, what the outcome was previously, etc. Beyond that, we begin to imagine how the present situation will affect us, and begin to dwell on the anticipated outcome before it occurs. Our thoughts can range from pleasant to unpleasant outcomes. Obviously, such thought connection can sometimes run away and lead to disastrous consequences. Self-fulfilling prophecies have a way of predicting what the outcome may be.

Self-Talk
Each of us is continuously engaging in self-talk or our own internal thought processing. If these are accurate and in touch with reality, we function well. If they are irrational and untrue, then anxiety and emotional disturbance occur and performance is disrupted.

Self-talk is best suited to enhancing and reinforcing self-confidence before an athletic performance. Developing a sense of control over the situation is critical to the outcome of the event. Self-talk can provide that sense of control if you learn to become aware of self-statements and direct them in a positive manner. You can, through self-talk, evaluate a potentially aversive situation as much less threatening when you have a sense of control over your own thought processes. Specific emotions such as fear, anxiety, or depression involve not only physiological arousal and somatic manifestation, but also how you interpret what is happening and what kind of labels you put on what is happening. This is self-talk or self-thoughts.

The interpretation you process is influenced by what you attribute your arousal and response to in the situation. As an example, if you are aware of an increased heart beat or muscular tremor, of increased breathing, of sweating, or desire to urinate just prior to a performance, you can interpret it as, "I am scared I am not going to perform well." This may lead to the self-fulfilling prophecy of that occurring. On the other hand, if you interpret this state of response to "I am ready and eager to perform because I can tell my body is ready and I am prepared psychologically as well as physically. I always feel this way when I perform well," then you have an entirely different "mindset" prior to the performance.

You need to become aware of what thoughts and self-statements are being processed prior to and during performance. You need to go over these and identify those that encourage and increase worry, and in turn, anxiety. Once you have identified those self-statements and self-thoughts that create worry, you need to develop strategies for changing them to positive and self-coaching types of statements and thoughts. In short, you need to learn to change negative ones to positive ones. As an example, you may be scheduled to play an opponent who has consistently outperformed you each time. If you are preoccupied with a self-statement such as, "I have never been able to beat this person before," you are preparing yourself to lose again in this situation. What you need to do is change your self-statements to something like, "I know I can beat this person. All I have to do is take it one point at a time. I have to concentrate on what is happening and what is about to happen. If I do this, I will be able to control my own game and my own performance." Then continue with, "I have practiced well and have worked hard to prepare for this match. There is no reason why I should not play well."

If negative thoughts interfere, dismiss them. Let them pass

on through and refocus on the positive self-statements that tend to provide a self-coaching voice for you. If anxious thoughts come, do not dwell on them but switch to positive ones. If this can be learned, situations will never develop into panic ones where you feel out of control.

Goal setting is closely releated to self-statements. When goals are made specifically for practice and for performance, they can provide the positive source for self-statements. If the performance goals are specific for the strategies and skills you plan to use in the contest, then your self-statements can focus on stating those goals in a positive, self-coaching manner. Through goal setting a plan for the anticipated strategy can be developed. This leads directly to forming self-statements that are positive and relevant to what you are trying to do.

Your attentional focus is directly related to self-statements. An awareness of what you are thinking about will indicate where the attention is focused. You can be taught to plan and practice what you want to do and to think before the competition. If you begin to get anxious just thinking about the performance, then practicing coping strategies such as relaxation, imagery, and concentration discussed elsewhere in this book will help you learn to stay under control. Practice self-statements and self-instruction which direct your actions so you come through the situation just as you would like to. You have to learn to become aware of and to identify self-statements which produce maladaptive behaviors and poor performance. With practice, this can easily be accomplished. Attentional focus must be internal and associative while developing these skills.

Self-Thoughts and Attitudes

Thoughts and attitudes are cognitive in nature. Perception and awareness of thoughts and attitudes leads to an emotional response. It is usually the thought that provides the direction and the control of that behavioral response. As a result, regulating your behavioral responses requires that you regulate your thought processes. This is a skill that can be learned through practice.

In general, attitudes are more stable and long lasting than emotions. All of us experience a continuous flow and interaction of having an attitude determine a perception which generates an emotional feeling leading to a behavioral response. Our behaviors and our performances are shaped by how and what we think of ourselves. If we think we can do it, we usually can!

Self-thoughts are much like auto-suggestions or self-hypnosis. Individuals can directly and indirectly influence their performance and behavior by directing their thoughts and actions through conscious efforts. Each of us must learn to "be aware but not aware of our awareness." There has to be a cognitive acknowledgment of what is going on without focusing entirely on what we are doing. It is much like the typist or the musician who loses the ability to perform effectively when the focus of attention is on what the fingers are doing. Or, like the centipede who could not walk when he was trying to concentrate on which leg followed which! When you have learned to execute the skill in such a manner that your body performs what it is supposed to do without any interference from your mind, the skill has been well learned. Only then can your self-thoughts be directed toward what is happening and about to happen. Physical skills must be learned and practiced until this level of performance is reached.

In general, thoughts can be categorized into groups: those irrelevant to the task at hand, those focused on the self, and those focused on the task. The thoughts that are focused on the self cause problems for athletes. When the self-thoughts are internally focused and consumed with a preoccupation of your own welfare and feelings, anxiety tends to increase. Perhaps the best description of this type of thought processing is "worry." The primary focus is on what does not feel right, on what might go wrong, and general negative thoughts. In this state of mind, you may become aware of minor somatic or physical complaints, either imagined or real. Thoughts may change to irrelevant ones that focus on imagined problems with how the uniform fits, the equipment, or bodily functions. All of these thoughts lead to anticipation of negative outcomes and expected failure and you soon talk/think yourself into a state that is counterproductive to any type of good performance. During this period, thoughts should be directed to the upcoming task and competition, not focused on the self in an internal, self-oriented fashion that disregards the event that is about to take place.

In general, when thoughts are self-focused, they reduce the ability to anticipate, interpret, and process relevant external cues and information. Worry about the anticipated performance begets anxiety! This anxiety is manifested in both somatic and cognitive ways as discussed in the chapter on anxiety. The tolerance to frustration and pain is reduced and you tend to become irritable and complaining. Performance errors are over-emphasized and interpreted as being more disastrous than they are. In fact, negative thoughts about the upcoming competition produce a greater disruption of performance than inappropriate arousal. Any highly talented, skilled, trained athlete can revert to a poor performance through lack of control of thought content. Not preparing adequately or not feeling prepared usually results in a poor performance. You have not prepared to win nor do you expect to win.

Many athletes develop a pattern of habitual thought that accompanies each competition. This is particularly true if the athlete has recently experienced a series of negatively perceived performances. Thoughts such as, "I never perform well in regional or national competitions," or "I hate playing so and so; I never seem able to play well against him/her," or, "I am getting worse instead of better; practice doesn't seem to help at all," are detrimental. If this type of thought processing continues, there is a real possibility that the negative appraisal of all efforts will generalize and become a dominant attitude. At that point, you will never be able to perform at your level of ability. You must learn to become sensitive to negative statement processing and change to positive statement processing which will help you reinterpret the situation. Self-statements and self-thoughts should all be directed toward building confidence and self-esteem. Further, you must learn how to distinguish the self-thoughts that are probabilities from those that are possibilities. Many occurences are possible; however, relatively few of them have a real probability of occurring.

You must learn to control the thought process so you can generate a mix of task-relevant content and mood-appropriate content to stay motivated enough to maintain concentration. Task-relevant thought content involves the thoughts related to what is going on, what is about to happen, and how you plan to respond to the anticipated situation. Mood-relevant thought content serves to keep you aroused sufficiently so that the appropriate psychological state is maintained in such a manner that the quality of the effort is controlled. In other words, you are involved, focused, and concentrating appropriately to maintain a high level of performance. With this control, you never become bored, detached, unaware, or "out of the game." If you do, you can refocus quickly and get back into action.

To stay securely focused on what is happening right now

requires you to learn the ability to concentrate without effort, to learn how to attend to what is going on at that point in time. You cannot be preoccupied with what has already happened, nor jump ahead in your thoughts and begin to anticipate what the outcome will be. If these types of thoughts do interfere and interrupt, you must learn to "switch channels" and refocus on what is going on right now.

Thought stopping

The ability to switch channels with your thoughts involves the skill of thought stopping, of being able to eliminate a certain thought. Thought stopping can help you prevent developing a pattern of thought that includes nagging worries and doubts which preclude a state of being confident. An athlete who is a "worry wart" is an example of an obsessive person in that he or she becomes obsessed with repetitive and intrusive thought patterns that are unrealistic, unproductive, and that generate worry leading to anxiety.

Learning the skill of thought stopping involves concentrating on the undesired thought briefly, then suddenly stopping that thought and clearing your mind. You can use a cue such as a timer bell, just saying "stop" out loud, snapping your fingers, or making a loud noise to interrupt the unpleasant thoughts. Thought stopping requires a high level of motivation and a focused awareness of your thought producing process. First, you must decide if you really want to eliminate a certain thought pattern. Next, select a particular thought that you really wish to extinguish. Close your eyes and try to imagine the situation in which you generally have that negative thought. Then, practice interrupting the anxiety-producing thought until you can eliminate it entirely. This may take some time to accomplish, moving from an external cue to command "stop" to an internalized one, such as thinking "stop" in your head. When you have accomplished this, practice substituting a positive thought that is relevant to the situation. Generate several alternative positive self-statements to use so the effectiveness of a single thought-statement will not be lost.

Accept the fact that thought stopping will take time to learn. The thought will return again and again and you will have to interrupt it again and again. Try to extinguish it just as it begins and practice switching channels to focus on another positive, pleasant thought. The more practice you employ, the less the negative thought pattern will reoccur. If you fail at your first attempt, continue to practice. If you have selected a thought that is very difficult to extinguish, then perhaps you can select one that is less engrained to begin to learn the process of thought stopping. Make sure that you begin by utilizing some external cue; when that works, then internalize it. Eventually, just the cognitive process will serve as a sufficient cue.

It has been rather extensively documented that negative, fearful, and panicky thoughts precede negative, fearful, panicky emotions. Learning to stop thoughts that lead to those states will reduce the overall anxiety levels and establish conditions where high levels of performance can occur. It has also been demonstrated that negative thoughts produce substantial physiological response; the body becomes tense and manifests anxiety somatically when anxious thoughts are occurring. This obviously disrupts performance.

Albert Ellis, author of *A Guide To Rational Living*, developed a system to counter irrational ideas and beliefs. The basic thesis of his system, called Rational Emotive Therapy (RET), is that emotions have nothing to do with the actual event. Self-talk or self-thoughts occur between the event and the response to the event. This self-thought processing can be either rational or irrational. It is the self-thoughts that generate the emotional response to the event. Only you can control your own thoughts and direct them in such a manner that you do not generate undesirable emotional responses. Following are four guidelines which will help you generate positive thoughts.

Guide to Promoting Positive Thoughts.

- It is not the competition or playing the sport that makes me nervous and anxious; the situation does not do anything to me. I cause the anxiety and fear because I say or think things to myself that produce worry and anxiety about how I will perform. I must think positively.
- To think that things should always be a certain way in a certain manner is to believe in magic. Situations differ because so many factors combine to produce the situation. To think that things should always be the same is to ignore causality. I must be objective and realistic in my thinking.
- We feel the way we think; therefore, we have to change how we think if we wish to change how we feel.
- We are all fallible. Accepting this within the framework of goal

setting procedures and allowing for short, intermediate and long-range goals, we can adjust to failures. When goals are met along the way, they reinforce us and sustain us over periods of failure.

Psychological Barriers or Self-Limiting Thoughts

Our beliefs and expectancies about outcomes have a great deal to do with the actual outcome of the event. Self-fulfilling prophecies are numerous in sport performances. It has been demonstrated that, as *beliefs* about the limits of our performance change, the *limits* of our performance actually change. personal excellence in any pursuit is largely a question of being convinced of our own capabilities. We must believe in our ability to attain our goals. At the same time, we must be committed to maximizing our capabilities. The degree of commitment is personal and must be worked out by each athlete. A thorough understanding of what the trade-offs may be and how to order priorities, short and long-term, must be reached as well. Wanting to maximize our capabilities involves the willingness to train hard and long to reach the desired level of performance. Athletes who do not maximize their potential either lack the necessary commitment and establishment of goals to attain it, or they have not learned how to cope with the perceived pressures of the situation.

There are classic examples of psychological barriers in athletic performance. One known to everyone is breaking the sub-four-minute barrier in running the mile. Until Roger Bannister finally accomplished it, no one was sure that it could be done. Once he had demonstrated that it was indeed possible, many other runners began to believe it was possible and proceeded to run sub-four-minute miles in a very short span of time following Bannister's successful attempt. Over 50 runners managed to run a sub-four-minute mile during the next two years. Weight lifters are notorious for developing mental barriers about how much weight they can lift, or believing that they cannot lift beyond a certain weight. Stories abound of manipulations of weight on the bar to "trick" the lifter into lifting more than he/she thinks possible. Once it is has been demonstrated that it is possible to lift beyond a certain point, improvement continues until another barrier develops. Psychological knowledge of what is possible has a great deal to do with what you can accomplish, particularly in sport. Believing that you can perform to a certain level, accompanied by realistic goals, can lead to maximal performance when all other conditions of training, equipment, and coaching are appropriate.

One consideration that must be accounted for in the whole concept of psychological barriers, or "sticking points" in your performance is your perception of how difficult the task may be. If the perception is one of great difficulty, then the knowledge that you are approaching the mental "pre-set limit" will be self-limiting. There appears to be variation in how athletes use feedback in terms of where they are in relation to their best performance. As an example, in studies of weight lifters where they performed under two conditions, one in which they had knowledge of what they were lifting, and one in which they were lifting without knowledge of the weight to be lifted, some lifters felt that the lack of knowledge of what they were attempting enhanced their performance. Others felt it was detrimental. Other attempts to manipulate the performance demand without the athlete's knowledge have produced similar results; some athletes do better, while others do not perform as well. There is a need for better insight and understanding of the role that one's expectancies for the performance play in the final accomplishment of that feat.

Awareness of Pain and Pain Control

There is hardly an athlete who has not experienced pain in one way or another. Pain can be experienced through effort and endurance, where waste products build up and produce discomfort, or by injury, which can produce pain with movement. Emotions play a strong role in perception and interpretation of pain. Some athletes may be so involved with an external or environmental focus that they are not aware of the presence of pain until their attentional focus is shifted to an internal one. Many athletes have been sufficiently distracted by the exercise or the sport activity that they do not acknowledge pain at all until after the event is over. Some may be aware of it, but are able to accommodate it due to the fact that their attentional focus is away from the self. A classic example of this was the Japanese gymnast in the Montreal Olympics who performed his still rings routine with knowledge of a broken leg. His attentional focus was obviously external.

We also know that individuals who expect relief from their pain get it. Basically, this is why placebos work. The cognitive expectancies of relief, or the emotional anticipation, add to the effectiveness of whatever pain killer may have administered.

Pain is relative to the individual; there is acknowledgement of the wide variation of pain tolerance that exists among individuals. There is also some evidence that certain personality types have greater pain tolerance than others. Further, there is evidence that team sports attract a biased population that tends to have a higher pain tolerance. However, within that biased population, there still exists a wide range of ability to cope with pain. One of the problems with pain is that it must be perceived and described by the individual who is experiencing it. There is no way that it can be measured externally. Further, what one perceives as severe pain can be completely ignored by another.

How one describes pain also varies from one to another, yet the physician is totally dependent on the description to determine where the pain is located and how severe it is. Some athletes describe it as sharp, or throbbing, or dull, or pulsating, or stabbing, or cramping, or as a sting. No one appears to be able to describe it specifically or accurately. All of these variations lead to difficulty in acquiring accurate knowledge of the experiencing of pain or the coping with pain.

A new medical specialty, orology (the science of pain), has been developed. There are now programs designed to teach individuals systematically how to endure and cope with chronic pain. Coping strategies are designed around cognitive control and learning how to switch attentional focus elsewhere. These principles work for athletes who are experiencing pain as well as those who live with chronic pain due to injury or disease. Basically, they learn how to regulate bodily processes and then how to "take themselves off somewhere else cognitively" so they disregard the pain. In short, they do not cognitively acknowledge the presence of pain; they are able to concentrate and direct their attentional focus away from the self to other thoughts. The principles are based on the total integration of the mind and body.

These principles are those employed by sword swallowers, those who lie on a bed of nails, or even an athlete who competes with a broken leg or a severe injury. Yogis learn these skills and, with years of practice, they learn to regulate most of their physiological functions beyond what has generally been believed to be possible. The basis of the skills rests on acquiring cognitive control, which develops with regular practice over a long span of time. The Russians believe that people fall along a continuum with some having exceptional control with little training, while others may train a long time and still not gain very much control. Again, this is support for individual variation that might be related to personality differences or to genetic differences (or both). At any rate, it appears that you can improve your level of control with practice.

Regardless of the control that you learn, there is a normal sensitivity to pain when you are not cognitively activating the resources and reserves needed to cope with the situation. It takes preparation and concentration with attentional focus to prepare for withstanding pain. One of the ways to begin to acquire control is to learn to focus on your breathing since it is always there. Practice breathing in a rhythm with the pulse at a 1:6 ratio, concentrating on the rhythm. As you breathe, imagine each inhalation bringing in energy to counter the pain; with each exhalation, breathe out pain. Repeat this several times with several minutes duration each time, ending with a long, slow, relaxed breath. Try to stay as relaxed as possible during this exercise and focus on "letting it happen."

Those athletes who are trained in autogenics and/or psychic-regulation techniques can apply their training to pain control. (See chapter on relaxation strategies for information on psychic-regulation and autogenics.) The ability to control blood flow, to alter skin temperature, to produce heaviness, etc., contributes significantly to self-regulation and pain control. With practice, an athlete can learn to bring on a sense of numbness, of coldness, or of increased blood flow in a very short time. Athletes can learn to increase blood flow and increase finger temperature fairly quickly with the feedback of a finger thermometer. (These are available from Conscious Living Foundation, P.O. Box 513, Manhattan, Kansas 66502.) With this type of feedback, athletes become aware of how much control they may be able to gain with practice and are motivated to practice on a regular basis to gain this control.

Team Experience 1

Provide a finger thermometer for each athlete. Tape it loosely on the pad of the middle finger with the bulb of the thermometer on the pad and the gauge visible to the athlete when palm is up. Provide several minutes for the thermometer to adjust to the finger temperature as many athletes will have finger temperatures that are less than that of the room. Make sure that the room is a comfortable temperature as well, as it is difficult to relax in a cold environment. Once the finger temperature has stabilized, have the athletes lie down in a comfortable position on their backs (see relaxation chapter). Instruct them to relax (they will have been trained in the techniques by this stage) and to concentrate on increasing blood flow to their hands. After 15 minutes or so, have the athletes check their finger temperature to determine if they have changed it. For some athletes who may have warm hands and a normal finger temperature, have them concentrate on reducing the blood flow and cooling their hands. Obviously, they cannot increase it if it is already 97 degrees!

Team Experience 2

Another interesting experience for athletes to increase their self-control and learn to tolerate discomfort is the ice water experiment. This should be conducted after training in relaxation, concentration, and imagery has been completed, since the experience provides a situation in which they can apply their strategies and skills. Because preparation is important in pain tolerance, you will tell them well ahead of the experiment what they will be doing and instruct them to come prepared with their strategies for coping. It has been well documented that those who set up their coping strategies in advance do much better in coping with the discomfort.

Provide a bucket with ice suspended throughout water of approximately six inches in depth for each athlete. Have them place a foot in the ice water and keep it there as long as they can. You might find you may set a time limit of 15 minutes for some athletes as they will have learned and prepared their coping strategies so well that they could stay there until it could become harmful. However, for those who pull out sooner, record the number of seconds or minutes they manage to cope effectively.

Those who withstand the discomfort longest are those who come prepared to engage in a variety of mental exercises while they are subjected to an uncomfortable situation. Each athlete develops his or her own strategies and they will differ from one another. When the experiment is over, ask each how he or she used relaxation. Some may have used imagery and put themselves on a hot beach or in a hot environment; others may have focused their attention on something entirely removed from the experience, such as working on a complicated mathematical problem, or playing music in their head. Others will substitute pleasant thoughts. In almost every case, there will be a switch of attentional focus from the self to something else outside. The application of disassociation, of environmental focus, or of external focus of attention, is the strategy to be used. The important fact is that the strategies have been learned and practiced well in advance of the application. This, combined with a positive attitude and a sense of confidence in the effectiveness of the techniques, will ensure increased coping ability. Athletes who have always relied on pain blockage for dental work discover that they can have similar work completed without nerve blockage after they have learned these strategies.

Self-Hypnosis or "Getting it all Together"

Athletes describe "highs" or peak experiences in sport that occur in a spontaneous fashion. Some have compared it to being in an altered state, of having phenomenal perception of everything that is going on around them. Others have described it as being in a "trance," or of feeling they are capable of accomplishing anything they wished to do. They report sensations of having exceptional energy, extraordinary strength, speed, endurance, and balance, all combined to produce a great sense of ease and "flow" of the performance. These experiences are sought again and again in sport. Somehow athletes feel that if they could reproduce these experiences at will, they would always be successful and able to maximize their performance. Hypnosis has been utilized in an attempt to reproduce these exceptional experiences, since one can experience "deja vu" under hypnosis. If it has happened before, it should be possible to experience it again, since one is obviously capable of reaching that level. However, hypnosis is not some supernatural phenomenon; you cannot accomplish anything under hypnosis that you are not capable of accomplishing physiologically. Hypnosis may assist in breaking through a mental barrier, a sticking point, or a lack of confidence that prevents you from doing either what you have done before or are capable of doing if you can get over that barrier.

No one has been able to explain the difference between self-hypnosis and the acquisition of self-regulatory skills which enables one to maximize his or her performance. Hypnosis might speed up the process; however, everyone is capable of developing his/her own potential and tapping the inner resources and reserves to perform at that level with training. Under hypnosis, whether the induction be by someone else or by the self, we cannot transcend our maximal performance; we only think that we do. The point is, if we learn how to develop our full potential by utilizing self-regulatory skills and strategies, we may appear to others as though we are in a "trance." In fact, the experiences that athletes have referred to as "highs" or peak experiences may be those where they were so focused, so centered, so "together" that they thought they were experiencing an "altered state."

As is the case so often, in order to "find ourselves" we go outside of our bodies for information about what is within us. We are guilty of ignoring our body's potential in the search for greater control and influence external to us. This search has led to drugs, alcohol, or hypnosis, but not one of them produced the "high" that has been reached getting one's internal resources together! In fact, the so called "altered state" may be the way human beings are supposed to function! It is just that so few of us ever discover our own resources that, if and when we do, we think it is an exceptional, extraordinary feat. In actuality, perhaps we should be able to bring this state into being at our own control. Perhaps this is *how* human beings are supposed to function.

What is the essence of this altered state? It appears that it is a combination of increased self-esteem, increased self-efficacy, increased sense of bodily awareness, the ability to focus and integrate function in a fine-tuned fashion, all with a great sense of ease and freedom! The sports laboratory may be the best teaching laboratory for all of these skills. Youngsters enjoy playing and they are highly motivated to do many things to improve their performance. Since all of the components of this altered state appear to be teachable, sport is the ideal environment in which to teach them. Even if youngsters do not continue on to a high level of performance, they will have learned skills that they can apply to everyday experiences for the rest of their lives!

Coaches and teachers can help young athletes develop the mind/body integration by teaching them to recognize the intimate interaction of the two. Athletes will readily understand how anxiety affects their performance, how injury affects psychological functioning, and how psychological functioning affects performance. Coaches need to understand these integrated responses so they can teach the necessary skills and strategies to attain them to every aspiring athlete. When mind and body are totally absorbed and integrated, the experience is extremely gratifying and pleasurable at any level of performance. When individuals, whether they be athlete or not, learn to tap into their own resources and regulate them, there will be no need for hypnosis in sport or for self-hypnosis. Each will be able to maximize his or her potential under self-regulatory skills and strategies without depending on anyone else! Just think how sport training could contribute to human growth and development in all pursuits if these skills were taught to every youngster early on in their sport involvement! Without a question, it would take time and practice; however, that time would be well spent and the skills learned would last way beyond the athlete's playing career.

Sport Amnesia

On some occasions, athletes appear to have selective or even total amnesia; they cannot remember anything about the performance even though they played exceptionally well. Some have misinterpreted this as being in an altered state. Because they were so highly trained and athletically capable, they could execute their movements without being aware of what was happening to them. A well-learned skill becomes automated to the point that it is no longer governed by conscious thought, but directed from some lower level of consciousness. This is similar to individuals walking in their sleep or even driving for a period of time while sleeping. The tasks are so familiar they execute them without any attentional focus.

Despite these facts, some athletes say, "I hardly remember anything that happened. I just remember the take-off, then I was in the water," or, "I only remember what I saw in the film after the race. I cannot remember anything about the race itself. It was as though I did not run in it!" When these types of experiences occur, it is difficult for the athlete to understand what went into that performance or how to recreate the situation so that they can perform at the same level again. Few athletes can manage superior performances while they are so highly aroused that they cannot process relevant cues. In maximizing your performance, the concentration during the competition should be such that your thoughts are continuously clear, active, and monitoring everything that is going on during the performance. In short, you are aware, but not aware of your awareness! You should be able to recall your performance in minute detail if you are free of worry and anxiety and your attentional focus is where it should be. On the other hand, some superior athletes do have the capabiity to produce excellent performances while highly aroused. However, these athletes do not have the consistency in performance that those do who are under control. Teaching athletes to control their arousal will produce more consistent performances over time.

The inner dialogue of the winner differs considerably from that of the loser before, during and after the competition.

Thoughts of Winners Versus Thoughts of Losers

The inner dialogue of the winner differs considerably from that of the loser before, during, and after the competition. As mentioned previously, your inner thoughts express different perceptions and feelings. These, in turn, have a way of becoming a self-fulfilling prophecy. All of the issues discussed in this chapter impact on helping you to process thoughts that are conducive to maximal performance. Making you aware of the types of thoughts you are processing is essential. Most of us are not aware of how irrelevant our thoughts are prior to performance or how self-oriented they may be. Once you are taught to control your arousal, you can direct your attentional focus to the cognitive processing that is continuously occurring.

Experience Directed Toward Becoming Aware of Thoughts

Keep a private diary or log of your thoughts prior to practices and competitions. This will help you direct your attention to what you are thinking. It will also help you recapture feelings and behaviors that were associated with superior performances, as well as mediocre ones. As you develop the habit of recording these feelings and behaviors before a contest and then relating them to how well you performed, you will soon observe a pattern of certain feelings, thoughts, and behaviors leading to superior performance, whereas another pattern may unfold that leads to a lesser performance. Acquiring this knowledge over time will provide a valid explanation for "having a good night." It will not be based on luck or on some mystical, phenomenal occurrence! You will readily see what type of preparation and cognitive state produces the exceptional performance. Then, with effort, these conditions can be arranged and directed as part of the regular pre-competition preparation. They may differ from one athlete to another, but in the long run, this procedure will produce far more consistent performances from all athletes. For more detailed instructions regarding the keeping of your private diary of your training and performance, refer to the guideline at the end of the book.

7

GOAL SETTING: THE REGULATION OF MOTIVATION

Coaches are always interested in learning of ways to motivate their athletes. Athletes need strategies to maintain their efforts in the face of all types of setbacks, slumps, off-season periods, and so on. Unitary concepts of motivation which originated in psychology such as instincts, drives, conditioning, etc., do not begin to explain one's persistence of effort in sport. Such theories have been replaced by other approaches to understanding motivation. Goal setting is one of those more modest approaches to motivation in sport training.

The Concept of Goal Setting

Goal setting is simply identifying what you are trying to do or to accomplish; basically, it is the aim of an action or a series of actions. In sport there are several other concepts that are used in the same manner as a goal. A performance standard or record can be a goal, accomplishing a certain number of points, assists, tackles, etc., or learning a specific skill, strategy, or progression can all be considered goals in athletics. In sport, goal setting is considered relevant to performance and therefore to behavior. The stimulus to your behavior has to be an internalized, cognitive one. That is, you must determine your goals in order to have the stimulus or motivation necessary to generate the behavior that will be needed to attain the goal.

Goal setting is viewed primarily as a mechanism for motivation. Your motivation is used to determine the direction the goal is set, the effort and the persistence of action to accomplish the goal. All three of these are influenced by goal setting. Basically, goal setting creates a focus of attention and action; it provides a purpose for your efforts. Different goals require different amounts of effort which are determined by the perceived requirements for the task. Persistence is directing effort over an extended period of time. In short, goal setting provides the structure for motivation which, simply put, is directing effort over a period of time.

Research in the area of goal setting during the decade of the 1970s has generated several conclusions. The positive effect of goal setting on performance is one of the most replicable findings in the psychological literature. The beneficial effect that goal setting has on performance is explained by four mechanisms of motivation: directing action, mobilizing effort, persisting with effort over time, and generating motivation to develop relevant and alternative strategies for reaching goals. Those of you who set difficult and challenging goals outperform those who set "do your best" goals or specific, easy ones. Obviously, you need to have the ability to attain or come close to attaining your goals. More effort will not produce the desired results if the goal is not a realistic one for you. You must also have some control over the performance pace, the approach and the methods utilized to attain your goals if motivation is to be maintained. Goals seem to motivate performance more successfully when they are stated in specific quantitative terms or actions rather than "trying harder," "giving 100 percent," "concentrating better," or "being more confident." Goals must be based on your own ability and performance.

Rationale for Goal Setting

If sport is to contribute to the development of social and behavioral values, you must experience success on some regular basis. Each athlete has the right to be successful; each coach has the responsibility to promote this right to be successful. Proper setting of goals and regular evaluation of the progress toward their attainment facilitate this right to success.

If you and the coach are to maximize performances both during practices and during competitive events, a common focus must be shared. This focus or goal setting provides a course of action for you and the coach for the hours of preparation needed for participation in competitive events. Without appropriate direction, numerous hours can be wasted because you have not determined a specific course of action for improving performance. The same holds true for the coach. If the skills and strategies that you need for competition have not been determined, the practice will serve little use.

Goals can be viewed as the regulators of your motivation.

Therefore, the importance of establishing goals cannot be understated. All dimensions of motivation, focus, the effort put forth, the persistence of effort, and the continued development of relevant strategies to reach goals, are determined by goal setting. If properly determined, goals can facilitate attainment of success for both you and the coach. What you and the coach are trying to progressively accomplish should be clearly delineated for training, for practice, and for competition. Each aspect of performance should have specific goals which indicate the purpose and the intent of the actions and motives.

Goal Identification

You must have the freedom to set your own goals, to choose what is best. When undergoing the process of identifying goals and ordering their priority, several key questions need to be addressed. How long have you wanted this particular goal? What have you done to date to achieve it? How close have you come to attaining your goal?. Why is it important to you to achieve this goal? The goal has to be put in proper perspective by determining your current level of performance. From that point, you and the coach can develop the program which will lead to the desired level.

Initially, most athletes express their goals in terms of "being best," winning, getting a medal, making the finals, or just making the team. Only later are they able to express them in terms of using their own performance as a reference point for evaluating progress toward their goals. Goal setting provides a systematic process for obtaining a norm or standard. Others view goal setting within the framework of athletic competition as being better than someone else, of getting more points and so on. The athlete usually feels good if a certain result has been achieved. However, the problem with this perspective is that intermediate goals are more difficult when the primary goal is a specific result. A "result" goal provides the athlete with little direction for getting there. Further, with only a result goal, the athlete is always attempting to reach the goal rather than achieving and continuing to progress toward more difficult goals. Setting a goal of winning does not provide for a specific course of action for winning. If the athlete or team does not win, efforts might be viewed as wasted since the goal was to win. Every losing effort should contain some goal success. Good feelings are associated with achieving a goal; as a result, one rarely has good feelings about the effort put forth or the progress made when the goal is only for the end result and that goal is not realized.

Another problem with goal identification is that any single goal will have several other related goals. You may have a goal of running a marathon in a specified time in order to prove that you can do it. Additional reasons may include becoming more fit or to experience running with many others who have the same goals. Other motivations (goals) may involve "hidden" reasons that are not voiced, such as impressing your friends, doing something most others have not done, justifying the cost of running attire, or justifying the time spent in training. Finally, when the result is achieved, there is a feeling of something missing if all the related goals have not been acknowledged. It is difficult to feel good about achieving something if you do not identify what you are trying to achieve.

Athletes who express their goals in negative terms such as not losing, not making a break, not missing a shot, not fouling, etc., should restate their goals in positive terms. Expressing athletic goals in terms of "I don't want to ...," have a way of becoming self-fulfilling prophecies. All goals should be stated in positive terms that can be evaluated.

In identifying goals, the current level of performance has to be evaluated. Goals are then set for long-term aspirations and performance level. The number of reasons available to achieve these goals and the rate of progress to date must be considered. You have to determine how meaningful these goals are. In other words, what degree of effort are you willing to put forth? How much time can be spent in attaining these goals? How committed are you to reaching these goals? The opportunities available must be evaluated. Are there limits to the coaching expertise, to the practice time available, to facilities, to the level of competition available, to financial support, to weather, etc.?

Coaches usually think they know an athlete's potential. However, many err in making that judgment. One of the ways to evaluate potential is to review the rate of improvement to date. Progression in skill acquisition should be evaluated on a regular basis. Individual progress should be noted because future performance is determined by past experience.

Criteria For Goal Selection

Once a goal has been identified, criteria should be established for the goal setting. Most importantly, the goal must be measurable.

Stating the goal in behavioral terms that are specific provides a framework for evaluating the progress. Both your coach and you should have a common base for evaluating the results. As an example, if you want to display "more hustle," how might this be evaluated? "Hustle" would have to be broken down into component parts that are specific and identifiable. In basketball, such things as stealing the ball, getting back on defense sooner, or getting more rebounds, could all be part of "more hustle" and still be evaluated in specific and measurable ways.

Goals need to be realistic, yet challenging. They should not be so easy that they are immediately attainable, nor should they be so difficult they may never be reached. You should be able to adjust up or down as needed depending on progress or lack of progress in the day-to-day evaluation. You may have to reprogram goals occasionally in much the same way computer programs are reprogrammed. If the desired results are not forthcoming, the program is not abandoned; it is just reprogrammed. You should not worry about temporary failures and immediately adjust down. You must evaluate effort before performance. If effort is being put forth, then success should result eventually. Performance evaluation is only meaningful if you are putting forth effort! It is important to determine the degree of success in terms of the progress, not the end result per se.

Both you and the coach must accept the goals that are stated. If goals are to be functional, they must have the acceptance of all involved. Goal formation should be a cooperative effort between you and coach, between you and team, and between your team and coach. The coach cannot establish your goals, nor should you try to establish goals without discussion with the coach. Then, you must accept the goals as they are stated. Individual goals should not be in conflict with team goals or in conflict with other teammates' goals. The guidance of the coach through coach/athlete and coach/team discussions of goals will be necessary to ensure that a conflict situation is not created. Individual, team, and coach goals must be compatible for success to follow.

All goals should be related to performances that are attainable. Goals must be individualized for each athlete. What an athlete expects, an athlete usually gets, or, what you set is what you get! Setting goals is a sign of intelligent planning, however, goals must be realistic. It is neurotic to persist in a goal and never abandon it if it becomes unrealistic. Each aspect of every goal should be related to performance and skill acquisition so that each can be evaluated in a progressive and systematic fashion. Goals are structured primarily to improve and/or maintain consistent performance.

When establishing goals, only a limited number should be stated. In many cases, athletes may want to set too large a number. Consequently, energies will be dispersed or less focused. Along with limiting the number of goals you set, consideration should also be given to establishing a priority for goal attainment. As an example, you may have selected three short-term goals; however, all three cannot receive the same amount of concentration and effort. In this situation, the coach can assist you in determining how the goals should be prioritized and which performance goals might be important to your performance level at this particular point in time.

Goals may be established for training, for practice, for competition, and for team-related performances. However, if you are overloaded with too many goals, frustration and failure may result. Goals should be pursued one day at a time!

Any goal that you set for yourself must be absolutely unique for you. You should not try to achieve something that a parent, an older brother or sister, or someone else has accomplished. Goals should be those that you wish to attain for yourself, not because someone else has attained them prior to you. If you attempt to attain goals that others have set or to use achievements of others as goals, there will be a lack of commitment as well as a lack of satisfaction if they are attained.

As you become more aware of the role of goal setting in organizing a sense of purpose for what you are about, it is also important to keep in mind that the achievement or lack of achievement of a goal has nothing to do with your own worth as a human being. Allowing your worth to be determined by success of goal attainment puts you in a position of unworthiness if you fail. Few can be successful in everything they attempt. In fact, you cannot continue to grow and make progress if you are unwilling to risk failure initially with your goals.

Many athletes avoid setting goals because they feel it will take the fun out of participation or that they might become obsessed with attaining the goals and lose the spontaneity of involvement. This is not the case; you can enjoy everything that comes your way and still have strong direction in what you want and where you are going. Having the ability to adjust up or down according to progress will keep the enjoyment in the pursuit of attainment.

It should be emphasized, consensus on goal attainment is essential for specific team goals. Without it, team members may not be attempting to attain the same performance outcomes. An understanding and commitment to group goals allows the team as a whole to accept what is expected of them. Each individual athlete will also know what is expected and how each athlete's performance is expected to contribute to the total team effort. When this type of preparation takes place, you will be clear in understanding what your specific role is in each practice and competition.

Types of Goals

The scope of any goal or combination of goals should be constant in direction. As indicated earlier, each goal should be of sufficient difficulty to be challenging but realistic enough to be attainable. Goal setting is dynamic in that you can keep raising your standards with progress in performance. The pursuit of goals is generally a mixture of successes and failures. Constant evaluation is necessary throughout the goal attainment process.

You should establish short-term goals as well as intermediate or long-range goals. Short-term or intermediate goals may be for a specific practice or competition. They provide the small, regular experiences of success and keep the athlete motivated. Intermediate goals may deal with a specific level of endurance or specific skills you hope to attain by a certain point in your training program. Long-range goals may be focused over an entire season, a scholastic or collegiate career, a lifetime career, etc. Athletes who train for the Olympics have very definite long-range goals that may not be attained for four years, eight years, or longer, depending on the sport. In addition to these long-range goals, athletes still need specific short-term goals from day to day, as well as intermediate goals that can be attained enroute to the long-range ones.

Beyond establishing goals on a short, intermediate and long-range plan, goals can be divided into segments depending upon the type of sport or competitive event. Some athletes may not be able to focus on such a large frame as an entire game. For these athletes, dividing the game into sections may be a better way of dealing with intermediate goals. As an example, an athlete might structure goals for the start, for the first five minutes of play, for the first quarter of play, and so on. At appropriate breaks in the action, re-establishing the immediate goals may take place. Athletes may find that this procedure aids in their concentration and requires their attention to be focused on the here and now and not on what has happened or what might happen later in the game.

How to Plan For Commitment

Goals must be for each individual, not for someone else. You must remember that you only have control over your own behavior. As much as you might like to change the behavior of others, you cannot. You must keep in mind that the only behavior that you can change is your own.

Beyond accepting that the only behavior you can change is your own, you must set reasonable goals. Commitment to attaining these goals is enhanced by certain procedures. First, you should talk openly about your goals with others such as coaches, parents, friends, teammates, etc. Making a "public" commitment enhances the probability of success. Putting the goals down in a written form also contributes to attainment. This written statement can be in the form of a contract or agreement with certain other individuals. Writing them down increases the clarity of the goals and provides a reference for all types of goals. Further, the relationship of one goal to another becomes more clear when they are written.

Starting a notebook with the written goal statements at all levels provides an accurate way of managing your goals. Chronological records are easily kept and can be reviewed. You learn to evaluate your own performance by keeping progress toward goal attainment. This is an important lesson to learn. In the process you learn to evaluate yourself, you cease to depend on the coach for regular feedback.

Perhaps the biggest bonus of keeping a written record of progress toward your goals is that of providing regular feedback. This takes care of motivation for the most part. An athlete who has clearly stated goals of all types after discussion with concerned parties, can follow the progress toward attainment without difficulty. The regular success that will be experienced with immediate and short term goals will provide positive motivation toward greater attainment. Success becomes a positive reinforcement for effort and for practice. Each day you should answer the question, "What have I done today to accomplish my goal?"

The process of goal setting is a cognitive one; however, the problem solving necessary to attain the goal demands creativity. Goal setting increases work output and effort significantly when compared to effort without goal setting. Further, goals are more likely to be achieved when expressed publicly. For this reason, communication should be public when discussing your goals as they relate to team goals.

Successful attainment of short-and intermediate range-goals help to sustain motivation to persist in efforts to attain long-range goals. The more clearly stated and detailed the goal, the greater the motivation toward attainment. You should have a clear understanding of what you are trying to achieve and how you are to go about achieving it. There will be relapses when you will want to abandon the goal or readjust down before it is necessary. When these situations occur, the goals should be restructured with more intermediate steps to provide opportunity to experience success more frequently.

The ability to set goals helps determine, in a fundamental sense, who you become as an individual. Goal setting is basic not only to what you wish for in athletics, but also for pursuing a productive and meaningful life on a day-to-day basis. One possible reason why things do not go according to plan is that there never was a plan in the first place. Goal setting provides that plan for athletic pursuits as well as other endeavors in life.

How Goals Affect Performance

Goals provide a course of action for you, the team, and the coach and give direction for the numerous hours of practice in which you engage. Goal setting can structure behaviors for practice, for training, and for competition. Athletes who adhere to specific goals are more likely to use relevant learning strategies to accomplish these goals than those without goals. Further, athletes who perceive these goals as being important or of having value for themselves in terms of their athletic performance are more likely to direct their energy towards attaining the goals. In short, goals which have been appropriately established by all concerned serve as motivation for performance when they are evaluated on a regular basis.

The research on goal setting outside of sport has demonstrated that setting objective, measurable goals that can be evaluated readily changes behavior. Specific life-style goals that relate to diet, rest, work habits, etc., can be incorporated into the specific performance goals as well. Research supports the notion that difficult goals lead to better performance than medium or easy goals. Further, difficult goals lead to better performance than goals of doing one's best or having no goals at all. More difficult goals produce better performance than easier goals because individuals work harder for difficult goals. Not only should difficult goals be stated, but regular evaluation should be provided to show performance in relation to the stated goals. Past performance has consistently served to predict future goals. You are much more likely to develop more confidence and to set higher goals after success. You tend to lose confidence and set easier goals after failure. Keeping a notebook of day-to-day progress is essential in monitoring the succession of successes and failures.

Goals affect athletic performance by directing attention and energy to the task, by motivating continued effort over time, and by the re-establishment of relevant strategies for goal attainment. If goals have been established challenging you as well as the team, little, if any, additional motivational stategy is needed. Goal setting allows you to assume the responsibility for your own behavior and motivation. Consequently, you can adjust and improve performance accordingly to attain individualized goals.

Goals also contribute to the establishment of better lines of communication between you and the coach, as well as with the other team members. Through the joint effort of goal setting, the coach and the athlete are better able to understand the expectancies that each has for each other. For example, an athlete may have an unrealitic expectation of playing on the first team or breaking into the starting lineup. The coach may expect this athlete to contribute primarily as a substitute. Inasmuch as these goals are not in a juxtaposition, a misunderstanding could result. The athlete, in expecting to attain first level performance, may find practice and competition frustrating unless there is communication about just what the expectancies are. Goals should be established that are challenging and congruent with the expectancies. Additional goals can be determined for attaining the long range goal of making the starting lineup. If the athletes and coach have not discussed mutual expectations, conflict situations, frustration, and resulting decrease in motivation will occur.

Difficulties Encountered in Attaining Goals
There are several hurdles that must be cleared before goal attainment can occur. Lack of necessary skill or skills can pre-

vent you from reaching your goal. Effort must be made to develop the necessary skill aquisition to attain goals. These skills can be stated in objective, measurable terms for short and intermediate range goals enroute to the long range goal. They may involve additional coaching and practice, watching more advanced performance, and so on.

Lacking the information required to achieve the goal is another shortcoming that prevents progress. Special goals for knowledge aquisition will have to be met such as reading to gain greater understanding of skills and strategies, talking to more advanced athletes to gain benefit from their experience and knowledge, or reading books on methods. In general, the knowledge necessary to participate in sport is more easily attained than the skills; however, both are critical to improvment of performance. The more knowledge you gain, the more effective you can become in practice and in integrating both the cognitive and the physical dimensions of performance.

You may have the necessary skills and knowledge and still be reluctant to take the risk of reaching for more difficult goals. You must be willing to chance a setback or risk failure in pursuing more difficult goals. For example, you may wish to change positions on a team and have the necessary skills and knowledge to do so but be unwilling to risk failure or perceived loss of effectiveness in making the move.

There are numerous other factors that create difficulties in attaining goals. Lack of coaching, lack of opportunities for high level competition, lack of facilities, insufficient practice time, lack of financial support, and seasonal changes in the weather are some roadblocks to attaining your goal. For the most part, an athlete who is motivated to attain a high level of performance can overcome most of the setbacks in one way or another.

For most effective goal setting, the following guidelines are helpful for formalizing and incorporating goal setting strategies and practice situations.

Specific Guidelines for Formalizing Goals

Just saying I would like to be a better basketball player, a better athlete, or make the starting lineup is not a sufficient course of action to enable you to establish goals that will help you achieve the end result. There are certain criteria which you should follow when establishing goals. In this process, you and the coach will put generalized ideas into some specific formalized goals.

- When establishing goals, *make sure the goals are ones that you established or that you and your coach established together.* You must make sure you believe in them and are committed to following the steps that enable you to accomplish them. Without commitment, the goals will serve little purpose.
- *Put the goals in writing.* This tends to reflect a personal commitment to a course of action that will help you achieve your goal. Also, writing the goals means that you think through the process that one must go through in order to meet the objective. It puts daydreams into a concrete course of action.
- *Goals must be challenging but attainable, measurable, realistic, and manageable.* Unrealistic goals or unattainable goals will create a frustrating and potentially failing situation. Goals must be structured in the proper time slot; some will be accomplished in shorter period than others.
- *When two or three goals are established, they must be compatible.* The attainment of one goal must not prevent the attainment of another. If you establish goals in two different sports, the goals must be compatible. In other words, you must have sufficient practice and coach time. Are the goals manageable and realistic? Can you evaluate your progress in a measurable fashion?
- *Goals should be flexible enough to allow for revision and change.* If the target dates are too rigid, you may not allow for circumstances which prohibit the goal accomplishment, such as injury, weather, or academic pursuits. Periodically, goals should be examined and revisions made if setbacks have been encountered.
- *Goals should have structured time frames or target dates.* Without the aid of target dates, there is no measurable way to determine your progress toward the behavior desired. Target dates serve as feedback and provide tangible evidence for one's efforts. Short-, intermediate- and long term- goals aid in structuring a time frame.
- *Priorities should be structured for goals.* It is not possible to achieve all goals at the same time. Therefore, you and the coach must determine which are the most important and which are the most immediate.
- *All factors related to goal attainment should be taken into account.* If you set a goal of improving your percentage of your jump shots in basketball, you may need to increase arm and shoulder strength in order to accomplish this goal. As a result,

you may have to establish goals related to strength building through weight training to attain your primary goal. Another example might be to increase your jumping ability. This might involve related goals of loss of body fat as well as increased leg strength to attain your major goal. Keep in mind the related steps that might be needed to accomplish your primary goal as you establish your plan for attainment.

- *Goals must be stated to allow for evaluation of effort as well as performance.* Success with regard to effort put forth may be attained before success in performance. This will provide positive reinforcement until such time as the desired level of performance is attained.
- *Goals should be related to the overall aim of performance.* All goals should be structured to improve performance or, in some cases, to maintain performance.

8

COMMUNICATION: LEARNING TO SAY WHAT YOU MEAN OR MEANING WHAT YOU SAY

Perhaps, the single most important coaching skill that needs to be developed is that of effective communication. Every coach and athlete knows the importance as well as value of having efficient and effective communication skills. This means establishing communicative behaviors and skills which can be translated and clearly understood.

Communication is dynamic and must be viewed as a two-way process. Communication involves sending as well as receiving and interpreting messages. The coach cannot simply send information without determining or evaluating whether or not the information has been processed by the receiver. Coaches usually have little difficulty in determining whether or not information about skill and strategy has been processed by the athlete as the performance outcomes can be immediately assessed. The task was either performed successfully or unsuccessfully. Other aspects related to athletic performance, such as goals and performance expectations, are not as easily communicated.

In athletics there is a need to develop communication skills which extend beyond the skill and strategy acquisition process. These skills should encompass an understanding of the expectations and goals that athletes and coaches have for each other, for the team, and for the sport. When communication is viewed in this manner, the athlete is considered as an individual, not just as a performer of sports skills. Unless there are open lines of communication where each individual is sending clear messages about the expectations and goals each has for the other, communication will be lacking. Team relationships and motivation will suffer along with competitive performance.

In examining the lines of communication, four major ones need to be considered. The first and most obvious communication line is that of coach-to-team, followed by that of coach-to-athlete, athlete-to-coach, and teammate-to-teammate. All four lines of communication impact on performance. If confusing signals or messages originate from one source, problems will likely ensue. What coach has not faced the situation of explaining how the starting lineup was determined or how playing time was determined? Many times major problems on teams can be traced to insufficient, unclear, or misunderstood communications between coach and team.

If the coach is to make a major change in the lineup, is that change discussed with the athlete(s) involved? In coach-to-athlete communication, taking time to make sure each athlete understands the rationale for the decision will erase many situations where misunderstanding or misinformation create turmoil or dissention. Athletes should not be left to conjure up their own rationale for why the change occurred. No two athletes will view the situation with the same degree of understanding. Communication will prevent many problems that disrupt team harmony and performance.

Coaches must create an environment which encourages athletes to initiate communication. Frequently, athletes have experienced the coach as an authoritarian figure who defies reproach. Communicating appears to be out of the question. Many problems in athletics can be traced to athletes who need to be encouraged to discuss their concerns with their coach. If you fear failure or if you have a teammate who constantly ridicules your performance, the coach must be informed if the problems are to be resolved. Athletes must feel that these communication lines are open without reprisal. There are far too many athletes who never communicate with their coaches because they feel their position on the team would be put in jeopardy.

Creating open communication lines among team members is also essential. Communications must be encouraged which are constructive. When the season is not going successfully, interconflicts on the team become more evident. Teammates may be using each other for scapegoats. Coaches must be aware that during these situations, communication may be detrimental to performance. On the other hand, athletes should be encouraged to work out some of their conflicts without coach intervention, if at all possible.

Communication Process

The process of communication involves sending a message to someone or some group and then assessing what effect the message had. In other words, as a coach or athlete, you have definite information you wish to communicate. The purpose of the communication might be for: a) persuasion, as in a pre-game communication; b) evaluation, as in assessing an athlete's performance; c) information, as in teaching a new skill; d) motivation, as in a half-time speech; or e) problem solving, as in dealing with team conflict. The information that you wish to convey starts in the form of an idea, emotion, or feeling and is then translated into a thought pattern. The thought pattern is transmitted through either a verbal or nonverbal channel or both. Using one or both channels, the message is directed to the intended athlete or teammate. The athlete receives and interprets the message according to the expectations regarding the type of message the sender might produce. The message is also interpreted according to the receiver's ability to understand the message content and within the framework of the previous communication.

Perhaps a coach has decided to instruct the athletes in a new system. In this case, the purpose of the communication may include three components: a) information, b) motivation, and c) persuasion. Motivation and persuasion would be included in the presentation if you felt that you had to convince the athletes of the value of this system over the old one. In presenting the information both channels, verbal and nonverbal, should be used to get the content across. The manner in which you present the information should be based on what information you knew the athletes possessed and how much information the athletes would need in order to comprehend the defensive system. Without some understanding of the processing level of the athletes, teaching a new defensive system would be useless as well as confusing.

Communication does not occur unless the receiver is affected in some way by the message that was transmitted. As noted, communication is a two-way process and imparting information of some type does not denote communication until there is a reaction from the receiver. If the skill cannot be executed by the athlete, one would surmise that communication for skill acquisition has not occurred. When the athlete starts to perform the skill and reacts, communication is occurring.

Coaches and athletes need to learn to read the reactions of each other. If numerous stimuli are transmitted, however, the signals may not be processed. Both the athlete and the coach may be hearing and seeing but not processing properly. Past communication experiences will influence current and future communication expectancies. It is important to consider these factors as well as goals, current status, and experience. The information must be relevant and meaningful if communication is to take place. The statement, "I cannot hear what you are saying because of the other messages you send" is appropriate here. All the signals need to be compatible and coordinated so the same message is being sent via all channels.

The communications must have a common base of understanding between the communicator and the receiver. Without this, communication problems may occur because the communicator assumes the receiver shares the same interpretation of the message. This type of misunderstanding occurs when the athlete believes he or she performed fairly well and the coach views the performance as being sub-par.

Components of Communication

When one communicates, two aspects must be considered. Firstly, the amount of information or content that is included in the transmission of the message. In other words, what was the intent of the message? Secondly, the content of the message, the actual meaning of the words being used, can be conveyed in different ways. The emotional elements in the message as well as in the delivery are critical.

The emotional element of the communication process includes the manner in which the message was expressed. What voice quality did the communicator use? Was the message intense, rapid, loud or softly spoken? Facial expressions and body language or movement also influence how the message is to be interpreted. The receiver does not process the content of the message without interpreting the emotional element.

Many athletes have experienced the irate coach who, during intense competition, demonstrates more emotional elememts than informational content in communication. The speech may become high pitched, faster, and more intense than under normal conditions. The communication pattern may be entirely different from that during a practice situation. Some athletes will have difficulty focusing on the competitive event or the communication of the coach when the coach's behaviors are inconsistent. Some athletes will find that the emotionalism of the communication may be more detrimental than motivating to their performance level.

Both elements, content and emotions, are important to the communication process but a balance between the two seems to be necessary for effective communication. Incorporating communication patterns which are effective is probably not a problem during non-stressed times such as practice or scrimmages. The stressed times of pre-game, competition and post-game require careful consideration as to the manner and content of the communication. It is during these times that the coach may lose sight of how much content the athletes can comprehend as well as how intense the message should be. The more important the athlete or coach views the competition, the greater the potential for increased stress to be demonstrated during the event and reflected in communication patterns.

Types of Communicating Behaviors

Much of our communicating behavior is habitual in that we do not give conscious attention to the manner in which we produce communicating signals. For instance, coaches give a lot of attention to the verbal communications such as instructional information, offering encouragement, and evaluating results but may be unaware of the behaviors that accompany verbal remarks. These behaviors may speak as loudly and in some cases, more loudly than the verbal communications.

Communicating behaviors fall into two catagories: verbal and nonverbal. The verbal channel of communication serves primarily to convey content or information. The nonverbal communication channel serves to support the verbal channel as well as communicating interpersonal attitudes. Interpersonal attitudes are communicated through appearance, gestures, bodily movement, facial expression, and spatial relationships. Nonverbal communication also serves to replace language, express emotions and convey information about the individual who is doing the communicating. One does not need the results of a contest to determine who won or who lost. The behavioral postures of the players and coaches easily distinguish the happy and elated from those who are disappointed.

Athletes and coaches are quick to point out specific gestures or nonverbal behaviors which reflect a certain attitude or feeling. A shrug of the shoulders, a facial expression, turning the back, or clenching the fists represent nonverbal behaviors which express feelings or attitudes with which we are all familiar. These nonverbal communications are interpreted in accordance with other communicating signals that have been transmitted—in other words, the situation in which the communication is occurring. A clenched fist may mean victory or anger depending upon which actions or signals precede the nonverbal communication. One can recall that the clenched fist had many meanings in the 1968 Olympics in Mexico.

Sometimes the verbal and nonverbal communication channels may conflict, that is to say, the nonverbal behaviors contradict the verbal or vice versa. Many times coaches are unaware of the more subtle communicating behaviors that accompany the verbal channel. In some cases that coaches or athletes may be verbally expressing encouragement but their body language may be displaying defeat, lack of concern, or disappointment. When communication occurs in the sport environment, both verbal and nonverbal channels must be examined in order to determine the message that is being transmitted. When athletes appear confused or misinterpret the message, the coach should examine the manner in which the message was transmitted.

Effective communication procedures in a swimming pool may not be as effective on the football or hockey field. No two sports and no two coaches will incorporate the same communication techniques. Coaching environments, coaching differences, number of athletes, and special relationships to the athletes determine that communication patterns vary widely. Coaches who instruct in an open environment may need to incorporate more nonverbal communicating behaviors than coaches who instruct in small or confined spaces with fewer athletes.

There is no one most effective way or best communication method or technique. The same message can be conveyed on many different levels. For example, encouragement can be verbalized as well as demonstrated by facial and body movements. Anger can be similarly expressed. Some coaching situations encourage more nonverbal communication patterns such as those of track, soccer, or field hockey. Whatever the channel of communication, it is important that both athletes and coaches share an interest in creating open, honest, and understandable communication which leads to improved performance.

Communication Breakdowns

In the athletic environment, the primary times for communication are centered around the scheduled practice time, pre-game, competition, and post-game times. During these times the coach and the athletes need to have effective communication. Components critical to the effectiveness of communication procedures are consistency, intensity, overload and positive components of the information. Other facts of communication such as attentional focus, misinterpretation, insufficient information, body language and negative communication contribute to communication problems.

Consistency of the communication is critical to performance improvement as well as building a creditable relationship. The athlete or coach cannot function if information given one day is changed the next day. Every coach knows the value of maintaining consistent information for skill and strategy production. However, expectations of an individual or team performance, which are more difficult to discern, may be telegraphed in an inconsistent manner. Athletes might assume that the coach is giving one message while the coach thinks another message has been given. As an example, based on all the communication signals, the athlete may be expecting to start the next competition. In the meantime, the coach thinks the athlete has surely gotten the message that the substitute role is a more realistic expectancy. It is important that both the coaches and the athletes establish communication patterns that are consistent across all situations. Each should become aware of how communication can change, depending on the criticality of the situation, and make every effort to maintain consistent exchange.

Closely associated with consistency of communication is intensity or how the message was imparted, what emotional tones did it have? Was the message presented in the same manner for both practice and game situations? Many times the coach may assume a different communication pattern during the practice sessions but during emotional or pressured situations, athletes may have to adjust to an entirely different communication pattern. Coaches who run practice in a calm and collected manner may resort to yelling or losing control during competition. Coaches may wonder why athletes can perform during practice and not during the competition. Some of the changes in the athlete's performance may be associated with the change in the communication pattern of the coach. When both consistency and intensity change, performance may also change. Some athletes will not be affected because they have learned to cope with the coach's behavioral pattern. However, other athletes may experience difficulty in making adjustments. In a stressed situation, the athlete should not have to make adjustments for the coach as well as the competition. If athletes are constantly having to adjust to and interpret what the coach is trying to communicate while adjusting to an ever-changing game intensity, attentional focus will be disrupted.

Information overload creates yet another communication problem. Determining how much information an athlete can handle in any given amount of time or situation is most important to the performance level. The coach must learn to limit remarks when there are time restraints or during pressure situations. Coaches frequently think that because time is limited, information should be presented as rapidly as possible. Little consideration is given to how much the athlete can absorb and assimilate. After such encounters with the coach, athletes may return to the playing field feeling as if they have been bombarded. Given so much information in such a short period of time, athletes may have only processed bits and pieces of the information imparted. Instead of returning to the competition with a definite focus or planned course of action, athletes may be distracted by trying to figure out what the coach was saying. As a result, their performance suffers.

Communication breakdown can also occur if the messages transmitted are always negative. Athletes need positive reinforcement for their efforts and information that is relevant to the situation and which contributes to the correction of errors. The athlete is the first to know when a performance is subpar or when a mistake has been made. However, coaches are usually the first to remind the athlete of a missed shot, a turnover, an error, or failing to carry out the assignment successfully. Positive communication rewards will almost always produce better results than negative messages. An overload of negative communication does little to aid in correction or to motivate the athlete. Being made to feel good about yourself makes you try harder. Knowing how to "push the right buttons and pull the right strings" through communication will inspire anyone to greater heights.

Other times when communications are likely to break down

in the sport environment are when players or coaches misinterpret or do not understand the message. This is most likely to occur when there is little time to provide information because the competition is in process. For instance, during the timeout in a basketball game, the athlete may have thought the coach said to give the opponent an outside shot when the coach was really wanting to pressure the outside shooter. Misinterpretation or not processing the information is a frequent problem under extreme competitive stress. If the information is not processed accurately the first time, there may not be a second chance to supply the information.

Nonverbal communications are also subject to misinterpretation. Not all behaviors are meant to be communicative. It is possible that athletes will interpret a behavior demonstrated by the coach as a message when the coach was unaware of sending signals. It is also possible that an athlete will intercept a message intended for another athlete. If the message is positive, supportive and reinforcing, there is no problem. However, if the message is negative the athlete may become preoccupied trying to figure out why the coach was dissatisfied, thus failing to focus attention on the ensuing action.

Infrequent or insufficient communication from the coach is also disruptive to the athlete's progress. When a coach has a large number of athletes on a team, it is difficult to make sure that each athlete receives regular communication. Some athletes demand more attention while others are not as open to communication. Obviously the same communication technique does not work for all athletes. Some athletes withdraw from sport when they are constantly overlooked and ignored. When any athlete gives time and effort to practice and training for a sport, the least the coach can do is recognize that in a positive manner occasionally. All of us need reinforcement to sustain our efforts over time. Make sure that you, whether a coach or athlete, provide support and positive reinforcement to others on a regular basis. Generally the "stars" and starting lineup get efficient communication signals. Those who need it most, the substitutes and those on the depth chart, are the ones who usually get little reinforcement. Some athletes perceive the coach gives all the attention to the stars and little to the remaining athletes. Make sure that all the participants get some recognition from someone each session. Coaches, captains, and "starters" can share in this responsibility.

Athletes need to know where they stand and how they are progressing. This means that they need some tangible feedback regarding their efforts and accomplishments. When feedback is not forthcoming, motivation ceases and the athlete becomes dissatisfied and discouraged. Individualized and appropriate goal-setting strategies will help alleviate some of these dissatisfactions, however, the coach and additional significant others must take time to help athletes evaluate their progress.

Communication is ineffective when attentional focus is somewhere other than on the task at hand. These situations are obvious when instructions have to be repeated or when athletes ask irrelevant questions. When an athlete is preoccupied with other thoughts, instructions are of little value. Learning the skill of concentrating and practicing "switching channels" will help to accommodate this problem.

If athletes or coaches make hasty or overly critical remarks, communication lines may close or individuals may not be as receptive to future communications. For example, if the coach has just reprimanded an athlete for poor performance in a harsh or unkind manner, further communication will be difficult. Further, the athlete will tend to react to the emotional tone of the message rather than the content. Communications which serve to correct or admonish a player's performance should be considered carefully and not expressed when the pressure of the competition is still in evidence. Too often players and coaches react in the emotional heat of the competition. Time should be taken to put the event in perspective before communicating a course of action. Reacting hastily and without thought as to communicative content and emotion can destroy trust and credibility, elements which are necessary for positive working relationships and performance improvement.

Open communication lines may not be established when athletes or coaches have negative or faulty attitudes. If an athlete or coach has a "mind set" about a certain situation or player, communication will be useless. The message will fall on deaf ears! Sometimes the coach will encounter this situation when teaching a new strategy or new defense. Athletes may be afraid to try a new approach and will have convinced themselves that the strategy will not work. The old way seems to work best for them. Lack of explanation regarding who starts and who sits on the bench creates poor attitudes as well. The bench warmers may not understand why they are not starting. In their minds, they are as skillful as those who are starting! If the coach fails to communicate the rationale for the starting lineup, attitudes of those who do not start may generate an avenue for conflict.

When the athlete has one set of goals and expectancies and the coach has another, communication problems develop. Goal setting is one of the best ways to open up communication channels between the coach and the athlete. (See the chapter on goal setting for further discussion.) Until a dialogue is established, the athlete may not know what is expected or there may be a conflict between what the athlete aspires to do and what the coach has in mind for the athlete to do. Early communication between the coach and athlete will help alleviate numerous misunderstandings.

All of us need work on our communication skills, as poor communication or miscommunication causes the majority of interpersonal conflicts and problems. We need to become aware of both our verbal and nonverbal signals and make sure that we say what we mean and we mean what we say! Good communication among all involved in the sport environment is essential. When communication breaks down between two individuals, motivation, commitment, and performance will suffer.

Communication During the Competition

Communication during practice creates fewer problems than during competition due to the emotionally charged environment in which competition generally occurs. Obviously, communication becomes more difficult when the athletes are not playing well or are losing the contest. When a team is playing well and winning with ease, communication is generally good.

Are there rules for communication during competition? Spectators can observe a variety of behaviors and messages being communicated by coaches and athletes during a competition. When all is said and done, there is little reason to have all this activity going on during the contest if the proper preparation has taken place prior to the game.

When athletes have been taught the proper skills and strategies, both mentally and physically, there is little that should be communicated during the contest. Coaching from the sidelines is not a very effective means of communicating to the athlete for several reasons. If the athlete has been taught to concentrate and maintain focus on what is happening and what is about to happen in the game, comments and instructions from the coach will not be attended to during the game. In fact, it is counter-productive to the athlete to continue to disrupt concentration and try to have the attention focused on what the coach is yelling out rather than what is going on during play. There have been literally thousands of situations where the athlete was "messed up" during the game because the coach disrupted concentration by yelling instructions.

An informal experiment was conducted during a basketball game which demonstrated how ineffective communication during timeouts can be. Prior to the game it was decided that the coach would call a timeout near the end of the game if the team was playing well and was winning with ease. During this timeout the coach was to have eye contact with each of the players and "mouth" some instructions without making an audible sound. When this was done, each athlete, without exception said, "Okay, got it." The point was made! Athletes do not attend to much, if anything, that is said when they are preoccupied and concentrating on the game at hand. Coaches need to develop strategies for communicating during these times so that they know the athletes are attending to their instructions. Athletes need to be taught how to focus their attention and how to switch channels from one focus to another and back when the situation demands. (See the chapter on concentration.)

There are times during the contest in certain types of sports where instructions are timely and appropriate. These can be given in an effective manner if the athletes have been taught when and how to deal with them. In general, yelling from the sidelines is wasted effort. It may make the coach feel better, however, most athletes will not attend to it if they are concentrating as they should. If the athlete does attend to it, it is generally more disruptive than enhancing to performance.

Strategies should be developed for communication during critical times in a contest. These should be discussed and practiced as a part of the preparation for the competition. There is no way a running commentary from a coach that is pacing up and down with the play will be effective communication. If this does occur, most athletes tune out the entire process. As a result, they do not attend to instructions that might be essential in a critical part of the game. All communications during the contest should be succinct, clear, and relevant to the situation.

Steps for Improving Communication Patterns

Improving communication skills is an ongoing process which requires constant attention and effort on the part of the coach and the athlete. Since it is probably the most important skill that the coach or athlete can possess, effort should be directed toward developing effective communication patterns which not only involve sending messages, but receiving and understanding messages as well. Several steps are listed below which will aid you in improving communication patterns.

- Athletes and coaches should be receptive to feedback. If the individual is attentive to the verbal and/or nonverbal communications that the receiver sends, you can determine whether or not the message was understood and processed. As noted, communication is a two-way process; therefore, messages are not just sent without attempting to determine the impact. Communicators should be sensitive to the manner in which the receiver reacts to the message. In coaching, information sent about skill production can be immediately scrutinized to determine the effectiveness of the communications. Areas in which the coach may not demonstrate that same sensitivity to an athlete's communications are goal setting and aiding the athlete in becoming the best athlete he or she can become. Learn to observe the receiver to determine whether or not the messsage was understood. Nonverbal communications provide additional insights into a receiver's processing.

- Individuals involved in athletics should develop open lines of communication. This means being receptive to suggestions and constructive comments. If a coach demonstrates a behavior which might be detrimental to the performance level of the athlete, would the athlete feel comfortable revealing that behavior to the coach? There is no question that the coach would communicate that to the athlete! Frequently, the communication line concerning coaching behavior has not been an avenue that the athlete would pursue without expecting penalty or reprimand. Athletes and coaches should create a communicating environment which allows for exchange in both directions without feeling threatened, inferior, or in jeopardy.

- There should be conscious effort directed toward improving communication skills, both verbal and nonverbal. Since athletes as well as coaches respond in different ways, there is

Improving communication skills is an ongoing process which requires constant attention and effort on the part of the coach and the athlete.

a need to determine what is the most effective communication method for each individual. When coaching team sports, coaches tend to communicate to the masses rather than to individuals. In some cases, this may be an effective procedure; however, it may not be effective for everyone.

Become more familiar with what your nonverbal behaviors are saying. Nonverbal communications may be perceived as expressing more than verbal communications. If coaches and athletes are not aware of what their nonverbal channel is saying, communications could be confusing as well as inconsistent.

- Do not assume that the communicator and the receiver will interpret the information in a similar manner. Coaches frequently address this problem when providing instructions to a group of athletes. The same instructions will be interpreted in as many different ways as there are athletes in the group. It is important to make sure the information is presented in a variety of ways so individuals who did not understand the first presentation have another opportunity. For instance, visual communication may be the most effective communication style for some athletes while others may communicate best by having the coach explain and then use some form of visual information.

Athletes may find that coaches jump to conclusions when responding to questions. The coach may have only heard the first part of the question and assumed that he or she knew what the athlete was asking. How many times has an athlete said to you, "but, that is not what I meant!" or you have said to to an athlete, "you were not paying attention!"

- Athletes do not need to be negatively informed when they have performed poorly. They already know it most of the time! Coaches frequently remind athletes when their performance failed to attain an acceptable level instead of examining the positive aspects of the performance. Critical but constructive comments are important for improved performance but coaches and athletes must be aware of the best and, therefore, most effective communication channel to be used. If a coach or team player is over zealous in performance evaluation, the athlete may be devastated. Performance evaluation must be handled with care. If appropriate communication channels have not been established, evaluation may be ineffective or disruptive to athletes and coaches.

- Be positive when communicating. Athletic performances are readily evaluated and athletes usually have some indication of how they played regardless of whether or not the team won or lost. Coaches should avoid yelling, insulting, and berating athletes. Although that seems like a common sense rule, it is amazing to see the number of times that coaches lose control in pressure situations or situations that are highly competitive. If coaches do not exhibit control, players quickly learn that they do not have to either. When coaches lose control, the emotional element of communication may override the content element. That may be the very situation where content is essential and critical to performance improvement. Effective communication does not have to involve making athletes feel inferior. Positive instruction can provide a constructive environment which enhances and encourages learning and improvement.

   It is important that coaches and athletes do not react hastily during pressure-packed situations. During stressful situations, it is difficult to weigh the impact of communication channels. It is during this time that good instructional cues are most important in aiding the athlete to focus on the components which will assist in performance improvement. Coaches sometimes rely on guilt trips or communications directed at making the athlete mad. For instance, "you are playing like a bunch of sissies" or "how can you let your teammates down" reflect the admonishments that coaches may use. If these are used, what kind of positive playing environment has been created?

- Communicate in a consistent and fair manner. Athletes need to be treated alike whether or not they are on the starting lineup or substituting for a first string player. Verbal communications must be consistent with nonverbal communications. All sideline behaviors communicate some message to athletes. Coaches need to understand that these behaviors may communicate more than they desire! Verbal behavior may not be compatible with what the athletes observe. The cliche, "A picture is worth a thousand words", is appropriate here. Become aware of all the messages you send on the channels you have available for communication!

- Prior to the contest attention to several points can enhance communication. While the coach should control his/her own mental state to keep performance maximized, much can be done to help the athletes' mental state as well. First, the coach should model the appropriate interest, intensity and arousal in the locker room during pre-game preparation and while on the bench during the game. Overloading the athletes with information and last minute instructions should be avoided along with distracting talk and references to interpersonal conflicts. Instead, communicate relevant information and task-oriented thoughts that athletes should be incorporating into their self-talk. Encourage the athletes to reinforce one another in a positive manner throughout the contest.

• Communications during the competition should be minimized to avoid disrupting the athlete's concentration. procedures for communicating during critical times in a competition should be developed, discussed and practiced prior to the contest. Every communication should be clear, succinct, and relevant. Attempts to provide instructions to every player during every play of the game is ineffective. Athletes have to learn to disregard the constant commentary in order to concentrate on play. As a result, they do not attend to instructions that might be essential during a critical stage of the game. The best rule is to keep communication to a minimum and teach athletes how to attend to instructions during timeouts and breaks in play.

9

STAYING ON TRACK:
AVOIDING OBSTACLES

Despite the best laid plans, things do not always stay on track. You need to be prepared for conflict situations that frequently accompany your participation in sport. Obviously, goal setting is the recommended procedure for identifying what you are trying to do or hope to accomplish. You also need strategies for maintaining efforts in the face of all types of setbacks, slumps, off-season periods, injuries or during periods when your performance appears to regress or remain status quo.

Commitment

Only you can determine the degree of your commitment to attaining your goals. Your parents, your best friends or your coach cannot tell you what your commitments should be even though many of them try! Without a question, the commitment necessary to pursue excellence in sport is tremendous in terms of time and energy. Many other things have to be given up in order to fulfill such a commitment. Almost no athlete reaches full potential without making a serious commitment and without sacrificing many pursuits that others are enjoying. Your commitment or what you want to achieve will be reflected in your goal setting strategies. Reaching your potential performance level requires that you assume a major role in your responsibility for your training, practice and performance. You alone must determine for yourself your reasons for making a major commitment to pursue excellence in sport.

When several thousand Canadian athletes of varying ability were asked why they participated in sport, four primary reasons evolved. The desire to master new skills and to improve their present level of ability surfaced and were catagorized under the general heading of need for achievement. The need to belong to a group, to have good social interaction with others was a second reason for participation. The sensory stimulation and sensations provided by the sport environment was another major reason. Adding a dimension of excitement, challenge, "flow," or risk, mixed with all the other things that can excite the senses in sport is an important aspect of staying involved. Having a sense of mastery and control over the direction and outcomes of efforts put forth was important to the Canadian athletes as well. Being able to make some choices and decisions on their own, being able to master some skills independently, and being treated in a responsible manner while assuming responsibility for their own behavior were important components in meeting the needs for self-direction.

Most drop outs in sport result from failure to meet one or more of these needs and desires. You must determine the priority order of reasons for your commitment to sport so you can establish goals to meet those needs. If the major reason for your involvement in sports is for friends, social interaction and belonging to a group, you may have difficulty in choosing a path which requires independent training. This does not discount the value of social support from teammates; however, you must be able to function independently of them in many situations. If your social group's goals and priorities differ from yours, the resulting conflict may interfere with your performance. On the other hand, if the group is supportive of your goals they can provide a positive and motivating influence.

Your commitment to achievement will determine how much you are willing to invest in time and energy for performance improvement. Achievement can be viewed as being either outcome or process oriented. Are you more interested in making the team or making the starting lineup than in attaining the necessary skills which might enable you to make the team? As was discussed in strategies for goal setting, you need to have specific process oriented goals for every practice and performance. If you can establish these steps, you will be able to evaluate your acheivement in terms of process on a regular basis as opposed to concentrating only on the outcome.

Goal setting is the basis of making choices and assuming responsibility for your own direction in your sports pursuits. As you can see, goal setting becomes essential to motivation, acheivement, evaluation and continued involvement. This cannot be emphasized too much.

Perhaps the most important aspect of commitment is to gain some positive feedback to sustantiate your reasons for giving so much time and energy to sport. In fact, if you plan efficiently, you will gain positive reinforcement and feedback on a regular basis. This, in turn, will provide excitement, enthusiasm, challenge, "flow" and all the other sensory dimensions of sport which make it fun. If your participation is not fun and satisfying or when the sport becomes more like work, there is little point in continuing. Most of us withdraw when our efforts are not rewarded in some satisfying manner.

Conflict of Interest

When you make your initial commitment to sport you usually do not know what other choices may appear down the road ahead of you. These unforeseen options and opportunities to develop new interests frequently create a conflict and require a continued renewal of commitment if you are to meet your goals in sport. Your sport priority determines how you resolve the conflict and how you allocate your time.

Practices may have been fun at first but become a drag because of time demands that take you away from other things you might like to do. You may find yourself debating whether what you are receiving from sport is worth the price you are paying. As you improve your skill and playing ability the coach may begin to demand more time. You will resent this unless you communicate with your coach and work out goals together.

Training expectancies cause conflicts as well, especially when they get in the way of what you would rather do. There is a sameness and boredom in training regimes that can only be countered with process goals and communication with the coach. Having to run a specified distance in a given time, perform a number of repetitions of strength exercises, make a specific body weight in order to play or similar requirements can be overwhelming without goals and communication. When a conflict arises concerning training expectancies some athletes give up attempting to attain them in a sytematic manner and resort to "cheating." Indicating task requirements have been met when they have not, or resorting to eating behaviors that are counter-productive and detrimental to health are forms of cheating. Anytime the pressure to meet certain training demands is in opposition to your current desires and lifestyle, you either have to compromise in some way or systematically meet the demands. If you are not willing to make the tradeoffs necessary, perhaps you should reevaluate your commitment and reasons for pursuing sport involvement. Coaches should also be aware of these conflicts and help you to structure goals and behaviors which will lead you toward that end in a realistic and non-threatening manner.

It is impossible to include all the potential conflicts of interest in this discussion. They will continue to occur throughout your participation. Keep in mind that you must reaffirm your commitment and revise your goals continuously. This, along with communication with your coach and others who are significant to you will assist you in meeting these conflict situations.

Information Overload

Coaches frequently exhibit the pressure they are experiencing by making greater demands on the athlete. You, in turn, will be bombarded with too much information, too many performance cues, and too many demands. At best, you might be able to process and incorporate only a small portion of the requests. Usually the greatest overloads occur during competition when the coaches react with a running commentary of instructions through the game. If you are really concentrating on your play, you will fail to acknowledge or respond to the coach's suggestions. Many coaches do not realize that they are frequently responsible for errors in play because they disrupt your concentration and demand attention to their instructions. Fortunately, not all athletes are distracted by coaching from the sidelines as some have learned to disregard these comments. However, this creates a problem because the coach wants your attention and response. Time for verbal instruction during play will vary from sport to sport and from position to position and have to be worked out accordingly by both you and the coach to avoid distraction and performance interference.

One of the most effective ways to avoid verbal overload during play is to develop short, concise cue words or statements. These need to be worked out with the coach during practice. If you find it distracting to be coached from the sideline during play, communicate this to your coach so a more effective approach can be developed.

Mind Sets

On occasion you might make the same mistake several times which creates a mind set with the coach who then may identify you as a "choker," "not aggressive," cannot handle the pressure," "makes mental errors," or some other label. In many cases your series of errors may not have been entirely your fault. Or, you may alter the behavior and correct the problem only to have the coach persist in the belief that your "label" is still accurate. If you continue to demonstrate play that is contrary to the mind set registered by the coach, you have a problem. You may have executed beautifully fifteen times to every one mistake, but that one mistake continues to reinforce the coach's mind set. As a result, you may get little attention or instructional direction from the coach. Communicating your concerns to the coach through the captain or directly is in order if this persists.

Situational Blocks

It is easy to get into the habit of blaming someone else or something else for our perceived lacks. In sport we tend to blame the official, the weather, facilities, teammates, or most anything other than ourselves for poor play. If you find yourself "passing the buck" you will soon feel that you have little control over your performance. You are not assuming responsibility for your play when you produce a whole string of excuses to explain why the outcome was not as you had hoped. Goal setting with regular evaluation of goal attainment will prevent this problem for the most part.

Plateaus in Performance

No one continues to learn and improve skills in a straight linear fashion. A natural learning progression involves some linear climbs and some periods when there is no apparent progress. After a period of time of continued effort, you will begin to notice that you are improving again. These plateaus in learning and skill acquisition are normal. You should not become discouraged when you hit a period of time when you feel you are getting nowhere. Just continue to set your goals, practice hard, and be patient as progress will be evidenced eventually. Athletes, like everybody else, learn at different rates at different times so do not worry about others learning skills faster than you. Use your own progress, goal setting and evaluation to determine how you are doing. You can also seek out the coach for evaluation of your technique to make sure that your efforts are in the desired direction.

Slumps

Batting slumps are perhaps the most talked about slumps in sport because they are statistically supported. However, slumps can occur in performance in any sport. Slumps are periods when the athlete fails to maintain the usual consistency in performance without any detectable mechanical failure in execution. Frequently the cause is related to one's mental perspective. That is, after experiencing a decrease in performance level, the expectancy is that it will happen again. The skill may not feel "right" even though no one can see any difference in the execution. Worrying about it not feeling right and not being up to your usual standard continues to sustain the slump or make it worse. Slumps may also be caused by physical problems such as fatigue, lack of sleep, somatic manifestations of worry and anxiety about things not related to sport, or a multitude of other reasons. Working your way out of a slump requires that you eliminate any physical cause and learn to disregard mental distractions. Using imagery and mentally rehearsing how you used to feel/see yourself at your previous high level will help. Letting it happen rather than trying to focus on too many performance cues is also a helpful strategy.

Staleness

Lack of motivation and attitude problems are generally at the bottom of staleness in sport. Boredom can lead to staleness as well. Utilize the goal setting strategy and add variety to practice and training regimes to increase interest and motivation. Improper nutrition, over-training and fatigue can cause staleness,so check your lifestyle and training habits to eliminate any of these causes.

Burnout

Burnout has become one of the "buzzwords" of the 1980's and is used to refer to a state when individuals become fed up with whatever they are doing and "throw in the towel." Burnout develops with chronic anxiety and worry about how you are performing. Finally, the trade-offs get to be too great and you decide to quit. It can also be caused by frustration day after day. In sport, frustration results when you never get to play, when you cannot detect any improvement, when you seemingly fail to get better despite all your efforts, or when the coach and significant others fail to provide you with any positive reinforcement. All of us need encouragement if we are to continue to put forth effort; without it, we tend to burn out. Some feel that burnout is just another word for depression; regardless, it is not a state that anyone enjoys being in for very long.

Practicing relaxation and working on your self-talk so you can get things back into proper perspective is a strategy that works for many. For others, removing themselves temporarily from the situation that has produced the frustration and anxiety is a solution. Many athletes withdraw from sport when their only feedback is negative and frustrating.

Rituals

Associating winning with a particular behavior or wearing a specific piece of clothing develops superstition or rituals. Coaches frequently wear their "lucky tie" or athletes may wear the same socks, necklace, ribbon, or some other "lucky" item to ensure continuation of their winning streak or lucky performance. Sometimes the association of this type of behavior with winning or good performance becomes so strong that the behavior persists long after a change has occurred in the outcome.

Eating a certain type of meal, following a specific routine hours before the contest, carrying a "lucky charm," wearing a specific uniform number or color and a multitude of other behaviors that have no effect on the outcome of the competition evolve because of the association with a cause-and-effect relationship. When these behaviors occurred in conjunction with a good performance or a win, the assumption that they had something to do with the win was made. You hope that when you repeat the behavior you will also repeat the results.

Superstition and worry about performance are generally the basis for establishing rituals which are followed prior to and during competitions. These rituals provide structure and routine in the face of uncertainty regarding the outcome of the competition. The more routine you can establish and the more familiar you are with everything that takes place prior to the contest, the more control you will feel you have. Therein lies the value of developing rituals and routines. They do not work because of some magic; they work because they help you to focus on the certainty of your preparation. They work because you can reduce all the unknowns before a competition to just one, that being the outcome to the contest. If you can do everything else prior to the game in a routine, ritualistic manner, you can focus all of your attention on the task you have before you.

Rituals are of value because they provide you with a

systematic procedure for preparation and serve as time markers for you as the competition nears. You can incorporate anything you would like into your routine for preparation. You can begin them as far in advance of the competition as you would like, hours or even days before. All the things that you do regularly in terms of eating, sleeping, dressing, stretching out, warming up and so on can be fitted into a regular, routine pattern. You can also include a systematic mental preparation of self-talk, concentration and imagery in your performance preparation. The more you focus on this regular ritual of preparation, the less time you will have to dwell on distracting thoughts and behaviors.

Dressing for the competition or for practice provides a perfect time for focusing your attention and preparing in your own private way for the specifics of your performance. Make sure you allow plenty of time for dressing. Follow your ritualistic schedule each time allocating the same amount of time for dressing. Keep all of your routine behaviors in the exact same order and focus positively on the upcoming event while you follow this routine. Keeping to this routine will provide you with a sense of consistency and control over what you are doing. Your pattern for regulating your arousal and readiness for the contest will not be left to anyone else. You can systematically check off each step prior to the onset of the contest and occupy all the time up to that point so you are not just waiting around with nothing to do but to worry until the competition begins. Make sure that you plan for all the time you have, leaving no time for distracting thoughts or worry to interfere with your preparation. You can use your rituals as your pacer for readiness and as time for reviewing your process goals. Establish a pattern that works for you and stick with it on a regular basis. Do whatever you find that provides you with more control, mastery and discipline in preparation for competition.

Losing

Inherent in sport is the fact that there will always be more losers than winners. Winning is easy to accept, however all athletes must learn to accept losing as well. Losing can be much more beneficial in many situations if proper evaluation of process goals occurs. Few athletes analyze their wins to gain a greater understanding of why they had a successful performance. However, most athletes will try to analyze their loss to obtain insight into why it occurred.

One of the things that an athlete needs to learn to accept is the fact that success comes in many ways, one of which is winning.

Obviously, no athlete plays to lose; each of us enters the competition with the attitude that we can be successful. We want to win. One of the things we need to learn to accept is the fact that success comes in many ways, one of which is winning. In sport we can be more successful than we have ever been in our lives and still lose the contest. Setting process goals and evaluating them on the basis of progress rather than outcome is one of the best ways to keep things in the proper perspective. In fact, if we plan effectively and set appropriate, realistic goals, successful performances and winning will generally take care of themselves.

A multitude of factors lead to winning. Being concerned only with the outcome reduces the satisfaction of winning. The attitude, "winning is not everything, it's the only thing" eventually leads to the attitude of "is this all there is?" Winning becomes "hollow" without an understanding of the effort and progress one has made to produce the outcome. Being able to evaluate your accomplishments in ways other than the outcome is essential to the enjoyment of the competitive sport experience. Learn from your loss; you can re-establish new goals that will lead you toward skill improvement. In the final analysis, you can frequently learn much more from losing than from winning!

Keep in mind that your self-worth as an individual is not determined by whether you win or lose! Athletes all too often allow this association to take place thus feeling worthless and depressed when they do not win. Being a winner is a frame of mind, and attitude; it does not depend on the outcome of the competition! The self-thoughts of a winner are in terms of performance which is consistently close to one's potential. You can evaluate your performance in terms of this standard rather than if you win or lose. If you do perform consistently at a high level and lose, you are in a position to analyze your shortcomings, revise or set new goals, and begin to improve your skills to increase your probability of being successful during the next competition. Your self-esteem is intact and you feel good about yourself when you can acknowledge your own efforts as well as those of your opponent. A positive attitude provides you with a sense of mastery, power and control over your actions. The energy that is generated by those feelings can be directed toward improving your skills. You know that you can do it with greater effort and hard work. A winning attitude is developed over time when you learn to set realistic goals and attain them. As this occurs you develop confidence about the control you have over your efforts. You learn to assume the responsibility for your practice and performance improvement.

If you do not allow yourself to fall into a "losing streak" you must redirect your thoughts and efforts. Not performing up to your expectations once or twice in a given situation is not unusual, however, when failure happens in a situation over and over again you begin to doubt your ability. Not only will you doubt yourself in that situation, you will begin to doubt your ability in all aspects of your performance. It quickly becomes a "self-fulfilling prophecy" and you get yourself into a losing streak. To regain your positive attitude you need to utilize goal setting and self-talk strategies as well as your skills in imagery, concentration and relaxation. While past performance may be one of the best predictors of future performance, it does not always follow. Only you can determine whether you can let your previous performance, good or poor, continue to influence your present and/or your future performance.

When Sport Is No Longer the Number One Priority

Does the real challenge begin when your involvement in sport ceases? Just stop and think of how much of each and every day you have given to sport participation over your lifetime! What will you do with this time? What will take its place?

When we are involved with organized, competitive sport much of our time is structured and organized by someone else. The time that we have left is spent in academic pursuits and the day-to-day responsibilities we all must assume to some degree. We go through this part of our involvement without having to decide what to do with our time. Most of your time, energies, priorities, goals, friendships, and thoughts are occupied by your sport in some way. Sport can become all-consuming, the most important aspect, and the only thing that matters in our life if we allow that to happen.

As we have mentioned before, you will have to establish priorities, develop commitment and set goals to pursue excellence in sport. At the same time, you must maintain some balance and cultivate some interests outside of sport. At no time during your involvement should you allow everything else to cease. First of all, there is no evidence that you have to give a 100 percent of your time to maximize your performance and reach the top. When anyone gives total commitment, other obstacles such as staleness, slumps, burnout, overload, and loss of fun and challenge soon follow.

How will not participating, not going to practice, not spending a great proportion of your time in the pursuit of sport affect you? What will you do with all this time you have not had for years? Some athletes find difficulty in adjusting to off-season breaks or post-season slow downs in practice schedules. They simply do not know what to do with their time and end up wasting most of it! For many athletes, it is the first time thay have had the responsibility of scheduling their own time and they do not know how to go about it.

Injury causes some athletes to have to quit "cold turkey" before they have given any thought to what they will do when they are no longer involved in sport. Many athletes who have not planned for this eventual occurrence resort to ineffective ways of coping with time that is heavy on their hands. Alcohol, drugs, gambling, depression, anger, hostility, resentment and a multitude of other socially undesirable behaviors surface. The only way to prepare for no longer having sport as your number one priority is to plan for that occasion! You can develop other interests, skills, abilities and friends outside of sport that will be there to take up your time when sport participation has been reduced for some reason. Those who have adjusted to this major change in their life with ease have been those who had prepared for a career by continuing their education as they participated. They have developed hobbies, other interests, and a personal life apart from sport that are easily expanded to fill the time normally spent in sport. You are the only one who can regulate and prioritize your life to maintain a balance in such a way that sport is not the only thing that determines your self-worth or consumes your every waking hour.

Regardless of how well we plan, you will face a period of adjustment during the transition. Only in sport can you be the best there is in the world at an age as young as fourteen! Most of us live with the reality that we will never be able to experience anything else in our life with the same degree of intensity, excitement or degree of involvement that we experience in sport. We generally have some goals in sport which focus our efforts and we generally make enough progress toward attainment to get sufficient feedback for positive reinforcement and motivation. To avoid a crisis of identity when sport involvement (whatever the cause) terminates, you must make sure that you cultivate all dimensions of your life to some degree during the time that sport is the number one priority. You can establish goals in other aspects of your life at the same time you are setting goals to maximize your potential in sport.

Establishing priorities and comitment is essential to pursuing excellence in sport. However, it is also important to develop other interests outside of sport. Too many athletes put all their time and energy into sport. They end up "putting all their eggs into one basket" and when the bottom falls out, they have nothing left. Develop other interests and other social networks outside of your sport world. It will add dimension and enjoyment to your lifestyle and put more balance in your involvements. If you are forced to leave sport or reduce your involvement for any reason, you will have other interests to take up the void in your day-to-day routine.

10

MONITORING YOUR PROGRESS

With regular practice of the cognitive skills and strategies outlined in this book, progress does not become evident for several weeks. It may require four to six weeks of concentrated practice for some athletes to detect noticeable differences in their performance. Many of the changes that occur are subtle and may go unnoticed unless specific attention is paid to day-to-day differences. It is important that you develop procedures and methods of monitoring your progress so that you can evaluate your accomplishments.

The questionnaires, check lists and exercises that follow are designed to help you determine where you may need to put forth more effort to improve. They will also provide you with a model or guide to adapt, modify and structure your own exercises to practice the skills and strategies that you need for improvement.

You might wish to respond to the questionnaires and check lists before you begin to practice the skills and strategies. This will provide you with some indication of where you are at the present time. Periodically you can re-take the questionnaires and use the check lists to see how much progress you have made.

Those exercises included here are only a start for you. As you become more aware of how these skills and strategies apply to your specific sport you will discover that you can devise your own exercises for practice. Once you learn the basic principles involved you can make your practice directly relevant to your needs.

COMPETITIVE BEHAVIOR QUESTIONNAIRE

Date_____   Name _____

Directions: Circle the number under the choice that best describes you. Answer each statement truthfully and in the manner which generally applies to you.

STATEMENT	ALWAYS	SOMETIMES	NEVER
1. I perform much better in practice than in competition.	3	2	1
2. Having important people watch me perform bothers me.	3	2	1
3. Before competition I have difficulty sleeping.	3	2	1
4. I worry about what others think of my performance.	3	2	1
5. When I make a mistake during competition, I have difficulty regaining my concentration.	3	2	1
6. I find that my mind wanders during competition.	3	2	1
7. I follow a specific routine when preparing for competition.	1	2	3
8. I make more mistakes when the pressure is on and the score is close.	3	2	1
9. I feel like I panic in close competition situations.	3	2	1
10. I berate myself during the competition when I make dumb mistakes.	3	2	1
11. When the coach or a teammate yells at me, I have difficulty concentrating during the rest of the game.	3	2	1
12. It takes me a little while to work out the butterflies in my stomach and settle into the game.	3	2	1
13. In important competitions, I am afraid that I will not play as well as I can.	3	2	1
14. Playing to my potential is very important to me.	3	2	1
15. I am a "clutch player" in pressure situations.	1	2	3
16. I am able to concentrate in a positive manner on the upcoming competition while warming up and waiting for it to begin.	1	2	3
17. I have my own game plan worked out in my head in detail.	1	2	3
18. I get nervous and worry before important competitions.	3	2	1
19. My thoughts wander out of control before competition.	3	2	1
20. I am easily distracted and irritated prior to performance.	3	2	1
21. I need some time to myself prior to a competition in order to mentally prepare.	1	2	3
22. I perform best when I know the specifics about what I am to do, when, and with whom.	1	2	3
23. The more difficult the challenge, the better I perform.	1	2	3
24. I perform best when I am nervous and worried.	1	2	3
25. I perform best when I am relaxed, calm and confident.	3	2	1
26. I mentally go over everything I can in preparation for the competition.	1	2	3

STATEMENT	ALWAYS	SOMETIMES	NEVER
27. When I am really concentrating on the game, I miss the coach's instructions called from the sidelines.	1	2	3
28. When things do not go as planned during the contest, I have difficulty concentrating on what is happening.	3	2	1
29. I enjoy competition more than practicing for it.	1	2	3
30. I perform best when my coach and teammates compliment me.	1	2	3
31. I can recall everything that happened during the competition after it is over.	1	2	3
32. I replay the competition in my head and see/feel myself playing as I would like to have played.	1	2	3
33. I set my own performance goals for each practice.	1	2	3
34. I set my own performance goals for each competition.	1	2	3
35. After the competition is over I feel that I could have performed better than I did.	3	2	1
36. If I could "psych out" my opponents, I would.	3	2	1
37. I worry about getting injured when I perform.	3	2	1
38. After a competition I think about how I played and what I can do to improve my next performance.	1	2	3
39. When the official makes a bad call, I let it pass and come back to focus on what is happening.	1	2	3
40. I make many trips to the toilet before a competition.	3	2	1
41. I feel weak and practically sick just before the game.	3	2	1
42. I try not to think about the upcoming competition because it makes me too nervous.	3	2	1
43. Just before the competition, I feel that I cannot remember anything.	3	2	1
44. My performance is consistently at or near my potential.	1	2	3
45. I enjoy practices more than competition because there is less pressure to perform.	3	2	1
46. If my mind wanders during competition, I can refocus immediately back to what is happening.	1	2	3
47. The larger the crowd, the more nervous I get.	3	2	1
48. If someone important to me comes to watch me play, I am more nervous than usual.	3	2	1
49. I think a lot about how I play and how I want to play when I am away from practice and competition.	1	2	3
50. I can see and feel myself clearly performing just as I wish when I mentally rehearse my skills and strategies in my "mind's eye."	1	2	3

Total your score. The higher your score, the more you need to practice the skills and strategies in this book.

Periodically re-take this questionnaire to see how much you have improved.

CHECK LIST FOR TENSION AND ANXIETY INDICATORS

SIGNS OF TENSION	CIRCLE FREQUENCY OF OBSERVATION		
	ALWAYS	SOMETIMES	NEVER
Facial grimaces, frowning	3	2	1
Clenching teeth, grinding teeth	3	2	1
General bodily restlessness	3	2	1
Moving body part continuously: foot, hands, knee	3	2	1
Headaches	3	2	1
Neckaches	3	2	1
Backaches	3	2	1
Diarrhea	3	2	1
Constipation	3	2	1
Irritable bowel	3	2	1
Indigestion	3	2	1
Irritable G. I. tract	3	2	1
Fatigue	3	2	1
Insomnia, disrupted sleep	3	2	1
Restless legs	3	2	1
Restless hands	3	2	1
Pulling, tugging on hair, moustache, eyebrows, etc.	3	2	1
Muscles twitches, spasms, cramps, tics	3	2	1
Excessive sweating	3	2	1
Cold, clammy hands and/or feet	3	2	1
Chewing fingernails	3	2	1
Chewing inside of cheek or lips	3	2	1
General irritability	3	2	1
Heart pounding or racing	3	2	1
Anger, hostility	3	2	1
Shaking hands, tremors	3	2	1
Irregular breathing rates, shortness of breath	3	2	1
Uncontrollable thoughts	3	2	1
Mental confusion	3	2	1
Forgetfulness	3	2	1
Skin rashes	3	2	1
Loss of appetite	3	2	1
Excessive eating	3	2	1
Unexplained fears	3	2	1

TOTAL SCORE_____

MONITORING MUSCULAR TENSION AND RELAXATION DURING PRACTICE

Sport _____   Name _____

DAY	Tension Levels		Unusual Feelings During Practice	Body Areas Tense After Practice	Experiences Causing Stress Today	Clear Signs of Stress Today
	Before Practice	After Practice				
1						
2						
3						
4						
5						
6						
7						

MONITORING MUSCULAR TENSION AND RELAXATION

GAME	Tense Feelings, Symptoms or Thoughts Observed Before Competition	Tense Body Areas or Muscle Groups	Signs of Tension Observed During Competition	Tension Level 1 (low)—10 (high) Before During After	Evaluation of Performance A B C
1					
2					
3					
4					

IMAGERY, VISUALIZATION OR INSTANT REPLAYS

The following exercise will provide you with some insight into how well you can use your imagination and control your imagery. If you dream in color you should be able to visualize in color as well. Read each statement then close your eyes and try to mentally see in your mind's eye the item that is requested. When the exercise involves action, try to see/feel yourself imagining you are executing the task. Keep a record of how successful you are in using your imagination each time you practice these exercises so that you can chart your progress in developing the skill.

	YES	NO
1. Examine in detail your favorite warm-up suit.		
Did you see it in color?	——	——
Can you examine everything before your mind wanders?	——	——
2. Inspect your running or athletic shoe.		
Can you see the scuff marks?	——	——
Do you see the colors and markings?	——	——
3. Visualize yourself going through your stretching and warm-up routine.		
Can you go through the routine in your head without having your mind wander to something else?	——	——
Can you feel anything in your muscles?	——	——
4. See/feel yourself running along your favorite route.		
In your mind's eye can you see things along the way?	——	——
Can you detect any sensations in your muscles?	——	——
Do you notice any change in your breathing?	——	——
Can you, in your mind's eye, reproduce the sensation of running?	——	——
5. Think about, re-experience the most exciting thing that ever happened to you in sport.		
Do you remember any details of the location?	——	——
Can you remember who else was there?	——	——
Do you remember what type of uniform you were wearing?	——	——
Are there any sensations of excitement when you remember?	——	——
Can you reproduce all the details of that experience?	——	——
6. Think about a skill that you are trying to learn or to improve.		
Can you see/feel yourself doing this skill?	——	——
Can you see/feel yourself doing this skill equal to or better than you have ever done it before?	——	——
Do you get a better understanding of what you have to do to improve your performance?	——	——
7. Think about the most recent mistake you made during an athletic performance. Now think about how you would have liked to have performed.		

YES   NO

Can you see/feel yourself completing the task without ____ ____
making the mistake?
Can you put yourself back into that situation and replay it in ____ ____
your mind's eye the way you would like to perform if you could
repeat it?

8. In your mind's eye, imagine that you are performing
successfully a skill that you would like to be able to perform
but have yet to accomplish.
Can you see/feel yourself getting through the skill ____ ____
successfully?
In your mind's eye, do you find that you fail at the same point ____ ____
you do when you actually perform?
Can you see/feel yourself completing the skill again with ____ ____
greater success than the first attempt?

9. Visualize your favorite room.
Can you see all the furnishings and how they are arranged? ____ ____
Can you see the colors and textures of the furnishings? ____ ____
Do you see the way the light and shadows fall in the room? ____ ____
Can you imagine that you are there in the room? ____ ____

10. Visualize your favorite food.
Can you imagine how it tastes? ____ ____
Do you detect any aroma that is familiar? ____ ____
Can you re-experience the texture of the food and how it feels ____ ____
to eat it?

11. Visualize your favorite fruit.
Can you visualize eating it in your mind's eye? ____ ____
Do you get any taste sensations? ____ ____
Can you re-experience the texture, the aroma, the taste? ____ ____

12. Think about a recent experience that you had that was
embarrassing or uncomfortable.
Can you re-experience how you felt at that time? ____ ____
Can you visualize all the details of the situation and how it ____ ____
evolved?
Can you go back in your mind's eye and replay that situation
the way you would have liked to have it occur? ____ ____

As you develop the skills of imagery, visualization and the ability to produce an instant replay of anything that has happened to you, you will discover that you can visualize everything. Practice re-experiencing situations where you did not perform as well as you would have wished. When you visualize them, see/feel yourself accomplish your role equal to or better than you have ever accomplished it before. One of the major reasons we worry is because we remember unsatisfactory experiences of the past. Using imagery, you can replace those memories with a better frame of reference in preparation for the next time you encounter that situation.

YANTRA

FOR CONCENTRATION AND IMAGERY

DIRECTIONS:
- Prop book up about eye level two feet from you.
- Sit in relaxed, comfortable position, close eyes and picture a warm, velvety black backdrop. Maintain that picture in your mind's eye for approximately two minutes.
- Open your eyes and look at the yantra for about three minutes. Continue to gaze at it without blinking and in a passive manner until you see an edge of color forming around the white square.
- Slowly transfer your focus to a blank wall. An after-image should appear as a black square. Hold that after-image as long as you can. When it begins to disappear, imagine it is still there.
- After it disappears, close your eyes and recreate it mentally in your mind's eye.

CONCENTRATION

"THINKING WITH YOUR MUSCLES"

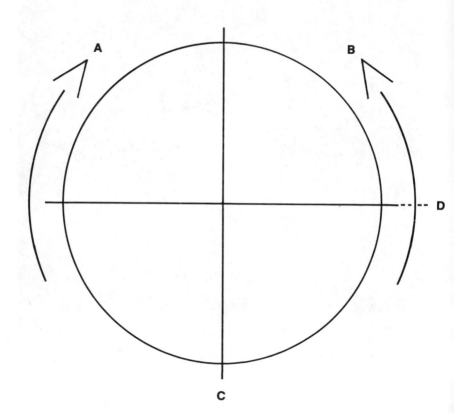

DIRECTIONS: **A**- Stabilizing the elbow, imagine the weight on the string moving in a clockwise circle.

B- Now imagine that the weight is moving in a counter clockwise circle.

C- Now imagine that it is a pendulum moving back and forth at a right angle to your body.

D- Now imagine that it is moving parallel to your body.

GRID
CONCENTRATION EXERCISE

Directions:
Beginning with 00, put a slash through each number in the proper sequence.

84	27	51	78	59	52	13	85	61	55
28	60	92	04	97	90	31	57	29	33
32	96	65	39	80	77	49	86	18	70
76	87	71	95	98	81	01	46	88	00
48	82	89	47	35	17	10	42	62	34
44	67	93	11	07	43	72	94	69	56
53	79	05	22	54	74	58	14	91	02
06	68	99	75	26	15	41	66	20	40
50	09	64	08	38	30	36	45	83	24
03	73	21	23	16	37	25	19	12	63

Comments:

SELF-THOUGHTS:
CHANGING NEGATIVE TO POSITIVE

Once you become aware of the thoughts you are constantly processing, you will become aware of how many of those are negative. The following exercise will help you learn to change those negative thoughts into positive ones which will provide you with encouragement and support.

Negative Thoughts	Change to Positive Thoughts
I can't	I can do it. I have done it many times before.
I won't be at my best because	I have done everything I can do to prepare.
That was a stupid mistake	The next time I do that I will...
What a dumb jock I am	I need to practice that more so I do not make that mistake again.
The wind is so bad I cannot do anything	The wind creates a greater challenge.
I am really nervous and anxious playing	The last time I played I felt this way and I played my best.
I am afraid that I will make a fool of myself	Unless I face the challenge and take the risk, I'll never know what I can accomplish.
I can't play my best without some help from my teammates	If I play my best and support my teammates, they will play better as well.
I don't want to fail	What is absolutely the worst thing that could happen to me? I could lose. If so, I will work harder to try to prevent that.
What is the worst thing that could happen?	I will be disappointed if things do not turn out as I want them to, however, I'll work harder to ensure success.
You stupid jerk	Why don't you try to do _____ next time? It might be a better approach than the one you are using now?
I don't think I am prepared	I have practiced and trained hard for this performance so I am prepared to do well.
I am tired, I can't go on	It is almost over, I know I can finish. The difficult part has passed.
It doesn't matter how hard I work or what I do, the coach never puts me into the game	I will ask the coach what things I need to improve in order to have a chance to play.
I am getting worse instead of better ..	I need to set daily goals and evaluate my progress on a regular basis.

Negative Thoughts	Change to Positive Thoughts
I have failed to get beyond this point every time I have faced it	I can learn from my mistakes. This time I will do what I need to do to be successful.
I don't care whether I win or lose	I have put too much time and effort into preparing for this not to put forth everything I can to be successful.
I lost again, I'll never be a winner	I can learn from losing. I need to talk with the coach to get some help regarding those things I need to improve.
I have no control over my involvement in sport. The coach determines everything	I have complete control over how much effort I put forth and how hard I am willing to work. I will work harder, maybe the coach will notice and give me a chance.
I will never be as good as	With more work, I can improve my skills and my performance.
It is not fair, I work just as hard as _____ but I don't get to play	I may have to work harder than some of my teammates to accomplish the same level of skill. I am willing to work as hard as I have to because I want to play.
The coach never pays any attention to me or gives me any help	Tomorrow I will ask the coach for some suggestions and guidance about what I need to work on to improve.
I never seem to be able to do this	This time I am going to think through and mentally prepare so that I can do it.

Every time that you become aware of having a negative thought, quickly change that to a positive one that will help you accomplish what you would like to do.

GOAL SETTING ACTION STEPS

1. My primary goal is _____

   _____

2. This goal can be structured into immediate, short-term and long-term sub-goals.

   A. Short-term goals are _____

   _____

   B. Intermediate goals are _____

   _____

   C. Long-term goals are_____

   _____

3. Additional goals related to my primary goal are:

   A. _____

   B. _____

   C. _____

4. My goals can be measured in the following ways: (How I know I have attained them)

   A. Primary goal _____

   _____

   B. Short-term goals _____

   _____

   C. Intermediate goals _____

   _____

   D. Long-term goals _____

   _____

   E. Related goals _____

   _____

   _____

5. Schedule for attaining goals—target date:

   A. Short-term goals _____

   B. Intermediate goals _____

   C. Long-term goals _____

   D. Related goals _____

   _____

   _____

6. Plan for attaining my goals: Procedures and steps

   A. Daily plan _____

     _____

     _____

   B. Seasonal plan _____

     _____

     _____

   C. Plan for competition _____

     _____

     _____

   D. Career plan _____

     _____

     _____

7. Additional skills, knowledge, opportunities, concerns, and the like that I have to consider in meeting my goals:

_____

_____

_____

_____

_____

_____

_____

_____

_____

_____

_____

EVALUATION OF PROGRESS TO ATTAINMENT OF GOALS

GOAL OR SUB—GOAL	DEGREE OF ACCOMPLISHMENT AND DATE	THINGS I NEED TO CONTINUE WORKING ON

NOTE: This record of progress should be maintained on a regular (even daily) basis. In this way you can continue to evaluate your progress and adjust your goal setting accordingly. If you develop the habit of keeping a daily log, you can incorporate your goal evaluation in that record.

Keeping A Daily Log of Your Training, Practice and Performance

The best way to determine your progress in learning skills and strategies that improve your performance is to keep a daily log of what you do each day. You will be able to look back over your record and see the results of your efforts. You will probably observe a pattern of behaviors and preparation that leads to a good performance or to a below average performance. In this way you can begin to understand that a superior performance just doesn't happen, that it is not just luck! You can learn to become consistent in your preparation for competition and include all the things that have led to previous good performances in the past, setting the stage for another good performance.

The first thing you should include in your log is your goals. Write down your long-term goals first followed by your intermediate and short-term goals. These should include all aspects of performance, training and other considerations that impact upon performance.

Each day you should record everything that you feel influences your performance in any way. Your daily training and practice goals should be stated and evaluated in regard to whether you met them or not. Keeping a dietary record is also a good idea, particularly if you are trying to reach or maintain a certain weight. You might find that certain foods have less than a positive effect on your performance when you keep a daily record.

Develop the habits of writing down your thoughts and feelings about everything involving your participation in sport. These include your reactions to teammates, coaches, practices, playing time, and so on. You will note if there is a pattern of negative thoughts and can begin doing something about them. You will also be able to determine if some of these thoughts and feelings are disrupting your performance and take steps to eliminate them. Recording these will assist you in learning how to change negative thoughts and feelings to positive ones as well.

A systematic record of how and what relaxation techniques you practice and when you practice and use them will also be helpful. Make a note concerning how your sleeping pattern is influenced by your relaxation skills. If you tend to experience headaches, backaches or other somatic manifestations of excessive muscular tension, keep a record of how these may be changed with relaxation training. You can also record how being more relaxed affects your performance at practices and during competitions. If you have nervous tics or habitual tension mannerisms such as continuously moving a foot, knee, jumping, biting your finger nails, chewing your lips, or whatever, observe whether you can begin to eliminate those with increased relaxation.

Monitor your improvement in concentration skills as well. Can you maintain concentration throughout a practice or competition? Do you find that you can read and study with greater concentration and gain more from a shorter period of time? Does your mind wander as much as it used to? Are you able to work for longer periods of time without distraction? Can you keep your attentional focus where it should be during competition without having it lapse? In general, keep a good record of your ability to direct your attentional focus, maintain it, and regain it when it does wander.

Your use of imagery, visualization and mental practice should also be recorded on a regular basis. When and how have you used it? What type of results did you have? Are you learning to maintain an image for longer periods of time? Can you incorporate or detect other dimensions (senses) such as sound, smell, taste, tactile, kinesthetic, or psychological? Have you been able to improve a skill or correct an error through the use of mental practice?

It is also a good idea to record other aspects of your personal life that you feel interfere with your concentration and performance. This will help you become aware of all the things that disrupt your performance and keep you from reaching your potential.

Each day you should evaluate your performance at practice or at competition so you can compare what you have done in preparation with how well you perform. In this manner you can determine the relationship of what you do and how you perform. You will see that you can develop control of your behavior as it relates to all aspects of performance.

It will take weeks, months and even years of systematic effort to really integrate and fine-tune all of the necessary components to maximize your potential in sport performance. The more you learn about how to control and master your responses so you can regulate and adjust your arousal to the optimal level under all conditions, the greater your confidence will be. Incorporating the cognitive skills and strategies with your mental practice will not ensure an Olympic gold medal, however, you can be sure that you will maintain a more consistent performance record and come closer to performing at your potential under any and all conditions.

THE AUTHORS

Dr. Dorothy V. Harris is a Professor of Physical Education at Penn State University where she serves as the Director of the graduate program in sport psychology. A world-renown sport psychologist, she is a Past President of the North American Society for Sport Psychology and Physical Activity. Since 1974, she has been an elected member of the Managing Council of the International Society of Sport Psychology—an organization she has served for the past six years as treasurer and membership chairperson. A prolific author and accomplished speaker, she has been acknowledged by *The World Sport Psychology Sourcebook* as one of four American leaders in educational sport psychology. With over thirty years of teaching, coaching and officiating experience, she has also served as a consultant to several Olympic teams.

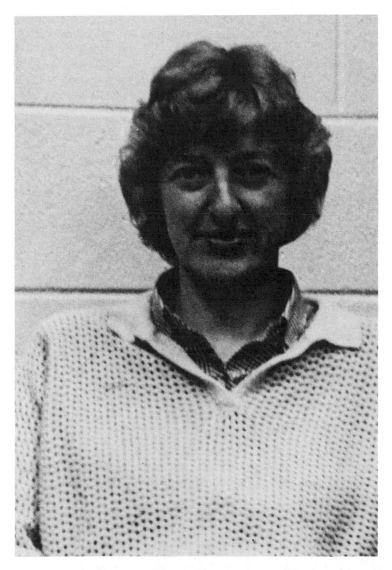

Dr. Bette Harris is an Assistant Professor of Physical Education at Longwood College in Farmville, Virginia. She has had extensive coaching experience, including over fifteen years at the college level. Currently, she is the head field hockey coach at Longwood College. She is also a nationally-recognized basketball official.

ADDITIONAL READINGS

Benson, H. *The relaxation response.* New York: William Morrow Co., Inc. 1976.

Brown, B. *Supermind: The ultimate energy.* New York: Harper & Row, 1980.

DeVore, S. & G. R. DeVore with M. Michaelson. *Syber vision.* Chicago: Chicago Review Press, 1981.

Gallwey, T. *Inner tennis,* New York; Random House, 1977.

Greenberg, J. S. *Comprehensive stress management.* Dubuque, Iowa: William C. Brown, 1983.

Hendricks, G. & J. Carlson. *The centered athlete: A conditioning program for your mind.* Englewood Cliffs, New Jersey: Prentice-Hall, Inc., 1982.

Jacobson, E. *You must relax.* New York; McGraw-Hill, Book Co., 1964.

Kauss, D. R. *Peak performance.* Englewood Cliffs, New Jersey; Prentice-Hall, Inc., 1980.

Klavora, P. & J. V. Daniel, *Coach athlete, and the sport psychologist.* Champaign, Illinois: Human Kinetics Publishers, 1978.

Loudis, L. A. & W. C. Lobitz. *Skiing from the head down.* Philadelphia: J. B. Lippincott, 1977.

Martens, R. *Sport competition anxiety test.* Champaign, Illinois: Human Kinetics Publishers, 1977.

Nideffer, R. M. *The inner athlete: Mind plus muscle for winning.* Ithaca, New York: Mouvement Publishers, 1976.

Nideffer, R. M. & R. C. Sharpe. *How to put anxiety behind you: Proven techniques for increasing mental productivity and physical performance.* New York: Stein & Day Publishers, 1978.

Orlick, T. *In Pursuit of excellence.* Champaign, Illinois: Human Kinetics, 1981.

Ostrander, S., L. Schroeder & N. Ostrander. *Superlearning.* New York: Delacorte Press, 1979.

Rotella, R. J. & L. Bunker. *Mind mastery for winning golf.* Englewood Cliffs, New Jersey: Prentice-Hall, Inc., 1981.

Rushall, B. S. Psyching in sport: *The psychological preparation for serious competition in sport.* London: Pelham Books, 1979.

Scott, M. D. & L. Pellicioni, Jr. *Don't choke: How athletes can become winners.* Englewood Cliffs, New Jersey: Prentice-Hall, Inc., 1982.

Suinn, R. M. *Psychology in sports: Methods and applications.* Minneapolis: Burgess Publishing Co., 1980.

Tutko, T. & U. Tosi. *Sports psyching: Playing your best game all the time.* Los Angeles: T. P. Tarcher, Inc., 1976.

Unestahl, L. E. (Ed.) *The mental aspects of gymnastics.* Orebro, Sweden: Veje Publishing Co., 1983.

Zaichkowsky, L. D. & W. Sime (Eds.) *Stress management for sport.* Washington, DC: AAHPERD, 1982.